Good Housekeeping

COMPLETE CHRISTMAS

Good Housekeeping

COMPLETE CHRISTMAS

All the recipes you need for a perfect festive season
plus original decorating ideas

EBURY PRESS
LONDON

This revised edition first published 1999

1 3 5 7 9 10 8 6 4 2

Decorating and craft text by Kristin Bjerkan

First published in the United Kingdom in 1999 by Ebury Press,
Random House, 20 Vauxhall Bridge Road, London SW1V 2SA

Random House Australia (Pty) Limited
20 Alfred Street, Milsons Point, Sydney,
New South Wales 2061, Australia

Random House New Zealand Limited
18 Poland Road, Glenfield,
Auckland 10, New Zealand

Random House South Africa (Pty) Limited
Endulini, 5A Jubilee Road
Parktown 2193, South Africa

The Random House Group Limited Reg. No. 954009

A CIP catalogue record for this book is available from the British Library.

ISBN 0 09 187256 1

PROJECT EDITOR: Julia Canning
DESIGN: Christine Wood
ADDITIONAL EDITORIAL ASSISTANCE: Gillian Haslam and Hilary Bird

Printed and bound in Slovenia by Mladinska knjiga d.d

contents

Countdown to Christmas

When planning for Christmas, perhaps the most important thing to do is make lists of things to buy. Here we have made it easy for you by providing you with the ultimate in Christmas countdowns, divided into weeks and then into ideas of what to shop for, cook and decorate. The potential heartache of Christmas can be avoided if you think ahead.

At this festive and family time of year, food plays a large part. So of prime importance are your Christmas menus. Before going any further, sit down with a pen and paper and start planning the various meals you will be cooking. In the rush to get the main Christmas Day meal planned, it can be all too easy to forget a lighter meal for lunchtime or in the evening, and there is also Christmas Eve and Boxing Day to prepare for. When you are planning your menus, bear in mind the following points:

- how many people you will be catering for
- the number of children that may be present
- if there are any vegetarians or anyone with other special dietary requirements to cater for
- achieving balanced menus; for example, make sure there are sufficient vegetable and fruit dishes, ensure you have some fish as well as meat, don't cook too many dishes with butter or cream
- that you have at least one or two dishes that can be made in advance and frozen.

Once you have planned your menus, write out your shopping lists – those items that can be purchased well in advance, and those that need to be bought at short notice. In the Planner, below, guidance is given as to the best time to buy all those necessary ingredients. It is also worth having a master shopping list pinned up in the kitchen so that you can tick off items as you purchase them and add other things as and when you think of them. In this way you will make sure that you haven't overlooked any vital ingredient.

EARLY NOVEMBER

Shopping

Buy your ingredients for the Christmas pudding, cake and any mincemeat that you are making.

If you are ordering turkey/game or other meat for your main Christmas meal, place your order now (see Buying Your Meat guide, on the right).

Writing Christmas cards always takes longer than you expect so buy them now so that you have plenty of time to write your messages. There are a great number of charity catalogues around at this time of year and as time can be a premium, it can be easier to order your cards from them now.

Wrapping paper, gift tags and ribbons can also be purchased from charity catalogues. As delivery charges are added to your order, the more you buy from one catalogue, the further the delivery charge is spread.

If you are planning to send cards abroad check postal dates now, so that you acquire and send them in time.

Cooking

The Sunday before the first Sunday of Advent, known as Stir-up Sunday, is the traditional time for making Christmas pudding.

BUYING YOUR MEAT

There is a wide choice of meat or game that is reared especially for this time of year. For the more traditional, there is the time-honoured turkey for Christmas lunch which is always popular because there is plenty of lean white meat to be had from this bird. You may prefer to eat a fresh, free-range turkey rather than the intensively reared and perhaps frozen variety. There are now also Conservation grade turkeys on sale reared in accordance with stringent standards and speciality birds like the Norfolk Black and Cambridge Bronze turkey which have a more pronounced and gamier flavour than the standard white turkey. Because these less intensively reared birds are produced in comparatively small numbers, it is important that you put in your order early.

You may want to consider eating something else for a change at this time of year. Fresh free-range geese, long legged or oven ready, tend to be available from late September onwards. Or how about eating duck or duckling (smoked varieties are delicious), or organically reared Scottish venison or beef? While some of these meats may be available at your local supermarket, it is better to ask a reputable butcher to order your requirements.

However, early November is just as good a time for cooking this delicious pudding.

As you are in the baking mood, cook your Christmas cake at the same time. Rich fruit cakes improve with maturing and by making your mixture at least six weeks in advance of eating can only be a good thing. Leave the baked cake in an airtight container and 'feed' it regularly until it is time to add the almond paste, icing and decorations (see One Week to Go, page 9).

Early November is also a good time to make your mincemeat. As it contains shredded suet it keeps well as long as the mincemeat is put into sterilised jars with carefully sealed tops. Store the mixture in a cool, dark and dry place. If you feel that you want to make the mincemeat earlier in the year, don't hold back – it will keep for up to six months.

Decorating

To make present wrapping easier, remember to collect strong boxes, tins, cartons and pots from now on. By thinking about containers now, you will begin to be inspired with decorative ideas for wrapping.

FOUR WEEKS TO GO

Shopping

Stock up with all the dried, tinned and packet ingredients that you will need over the holiday. Almond paste and icing sugar, for example, can quickly run out in the shops. Buy a little more than you think you will need in case of accidents. Keep an eye out for white almond paste as it is a better buy than the yellow variety which can look a little garish.

Make space for all these extra purchases by clearing out your storage spaces, removing all the old, almost empty or redundant tins and packets. You will also discover in good time whether basic ingredients like flour and salt, for example, need replenishing; or if you have, say, sufficient cornflour and custard mix already.

Here is a checklist of the ingredients you are most likely to need:

almond paste
bread mix
breakfast cereals
cake decorations
cornflour
cranberry sauce
crisps, olives and other snacks
custard – powdered/canned
dried/glacé fruits
essences and flavourings, such as vanilla and almond
flour – self-raising, plain, wholemeal
fruit juice – long-life cartons/jars
gelatine
golden syrup
horseradish sauce
jam
marmalade
milk – long life
mustard
nuts – such as peanuts and cashews
oils – olive, vegetable, sunflower, walnut
pasta
pastry – filo, flaky, puff, shortcrust
pulses
redcurrant jelly
rice
salt
spices – such as nutmeg, cinnamon and cloves
stock cubes
sugar – granulated, caster, icing
suet
tomato purée/paste
treacle
vinegar
yeast – dried

If you are making your own Christmas cards, buy the card, envelopes and any decorative devices you need. Cards that are being sent to international destinations need to be written especially early.

Keep an eye open for basic craft items – it is well worth having a stock of this sort of thing because once you start making Christmas decorations you will find that all sorts of ideas spring to mind. Here is a list of the things that you might need:

decorative papers for tags or name cards
double-sided tape
fabric paints
glitter glue
glue
gold and silver pens and paint sprays
oasis balls and/or wreaths for dried flowers
polystyrene balls – available in different sizes
raffia

ribbons – plain, patterned, and in various widths
scissors – make sure these are paper-cutting scissors and sharp, and not someone's best fabric cutting shears as paper can ruin them
spray glue
stamp designs
stencils – such as stars, bells and Santa Claus
sticky tape
twig wreath, ball or basket
twines – such as plain, gold and silver

Keep all these things in a box so that they remain together and are easy to carry from room to room as required.

Cooking
Start cooking any of your proposed dishes that can be put in the freezer. It is especially worth making mince pies in batches so that you don't have to handle too much pastry at one time. If you don't want to make your own mincemeat, you can easily doctor ready-made mincemeat by adding some finely chopped apple, dried apricots, nuts and some brandy to enliven it.

Decorating
Start thinking about how you are going to decorate the home – look at pages 13-55 for ideas and, for additional inspiration, scan magazines or just look at the ways in which shop windows are decorated. You will soon glean all sorts of ways to make pretty decorations for the tree, fireplace, Christmas table, or to hang in your windows. If there are specific requirements, buy these items now and keep them in your container with the other decorating essentials until it is time to put your creative talents to full use.

THREE WEEKS TO GO

Shopping
Now that you have purchased all your store cupboard basics, turn your mind to non-food shopping. It is better to break your shopping trips into smaller lists like this as it is both kinder to your purse and your arms – dragging two trolleys around a supermarket can be very hard work. Here is a list of the items that you might want to consider:

baby food
baking parchment
batteries
cake boards
cake decorations
candles
cards
cling film
cocktail sticks
crackers
dustbin liners
freezer bags
fuses
greaseproof paper
ice-cube bags
kitchen bin liners
kitchen foil, wide enough for the turkey
kitchen roll
matches
mince pie tins
paper napkins/plates/cups
paper tablecloth(s)
party streamers
pastry cutters – round and shaped, such as star, holly and reindeer
pet food

rice paper
roasting tin for turkey
spare light bulbs for the house and Christmas tree
toilet paper

Cooking

Edible gifts make wonderful presents but to save you the stress of having to make them nearer Christmas look for ideas that will keep well in jars, like pickles, chutneys and preserves, or items that survive a few weeks in a refrigerator or can be frozen, such as glacéed fruits and chocolates.

Ice-cube bags are an incredibly practical invention, and as soon as you have bought your bags, fill them up so that you have a well-stocked freezer. Christmas is a time when friends and family decide to pop in at unexpected moments and so it is as well to be prepared with this sort of item, then you will have instantly chilled drinks to hand.

With the advent of the ice-cube bag, ice-cube trays are all too frequently made redundant. Don't throw them away, however, they are the perfect way to store your fresh herbs. Simply chop them up and freeze them in water in the ice-cube trays.

Decorating

Paper tablecloths are certainly fuss free and there is a wide choice available at this time of year. When you are choosing yours, make sure you buy something that blends in well with your china and cutlery. For example, blue always looks good with silver and red with copper and gold. Choose napkins to match at the same time.

Plan your other table decorations at the same time so that you know you will have a beautifully coordinated setting and you will have the time to search around for any special items such as candles in a particular colour. For more ideas on creating the look you want for your table, see pages 37-49.

DRINKS PARTY

If you are planning to hold a drinks party, order your drinks and glasses well in advance. Many wine warehouses, off-licences and supermarkets will supply glasses and ice with a drinks order. Take them up on this – lots of ice is essential for cooling alcoholic and soft drinks. An easy way to chill bottles is to place them in bins filled with ice.

- Allow half a bottle of wine per person or if you are making a punch or mulled wine, 3-4 glasses.
- Remember to order soft drinks.
- When planning the food, allow 8-10 canapés per person unless your guests are going on to eat elsewhere, in which case 5 bites should be sufficient.
- If you are having lots of guests if may be worth hiring waiters or waitresses to take some of the strain. A professional help can cope with about 25 guests, untrained would manage 15 guests.

TWO WEEKS TO GO

Shopping

Now it is time to turn your mind to the drinks that are likely to be consumed over Christmas. Here is a suggested list:

beer
cider
fizzy drinks
fruit juices/cordials/nectars
lager – including low-alcohol or alcohol-free
liqueurs
mineral water
mixers – such as ginger ale, soda water and tonic
spirits – such as brandy, gin, rum and whisky
wines – fortified, low-alcohol, red, sparkling, white

When choosing your wines, remember that the rich, spicy trimmings on the turkey can easily overwhelm such classic French wines as claret and burgundy. So look for a reasonably priced New World red; Californian Cabernet Sauvignon or robust Chilean Cabernet. If you prefer white wine, look for a fresh and fruity wine such as an Australian Chardonnay. For a pudding wine, it is hard to beat a traditional Madeira.

When buying low-alcohol or alcohol-free lager, check the labelling carefully to ensure that you are purchasing exactly what you want – remember that low-alcohol lager contains a percentage of alcohol.

If storing all these large bottles and boxes is a problem, put them outside the back door, if you are sure they won't disappear. However, beware of a heavy frost at night which would make the bottles explode.

Cooking

Brandy butter will keep in the refrigerator for up to two weeks, so why not make it now so that there is one less thing to think of next week?

Likewise, croûtons keep well in a sealed jar or tin, as do breadcrumbs.

Decorating

Start wrapping your Christmas presents. This can be a surprisingly time consuming task and the longer you have to do it, the better. You may also find when you begin that you will start getting other decorative ideas and want to buy extra bits and pieces.

Check that your Christmas tree lights work so that if necessary you can buy some more bulbs. It is also worth ensuring that your glass baubles are still in one piece and that you have sufficient for this year. If not, you might want to consider buying some more.

While you are checking things, make sure that your tablecloth and napkins are clean and still well-pressed.

ONE WEEK TO GO

Shopping

To prevent too many last-minute panics, buy what you need from the following. There will no doubt be other things you would like to add to the list:

bacon
biscuits – sweet and savoury
cheese
chocolates
coffee/tea plus filter papers if necessary
bread – ready-to-bake or fresh for freezer storage
eggs
nuts – whole
trifle sponges
yogurts and fromage frais (check the date stamps)

Buy any flowers and foliage that you need for the table centrepiece or other arrangements you are considering. Don't leave this too late or the shops could be sold out. To ensure that the flowers last well into the holiday, choose flowers with buds as tightly shut as possible and when you get them home, put them into a bucket of fresh water, first trimming off 2.5 cm (1 inch) of stem with a sharp knife so that the flow of water up the stems is not impeded in any way. Then keep the bucket in a cool, dark room until you are ready to make your arrangements.

Also buy any oasis that you may need. This is available as bricks, balls or wreaths so decide on your requirements before purchasing.

Bring in your Christmas tree from the garden or buy one. If you have the space in the garden to grow a tree, consider buying one with a root ball. For more information on making the most of your tree, see page 26.

Cooking

Put almond paste on the cake. Leave for up to two days and then put on the fondant icing. This icing needs a day or so to dry before you add the final decorative touches; cover it with greaseproof paper to protect the icing.

It is as well to decide on what stuffing you will be using so that you can plan your ingredients accordingly.

Decorating

When you choose to decorate your house is an entirely personal decision. Some people like to leave it as late as Christmas Eve, whereas others like to make the most of the decorations and start filling the house both inside and out up to two weeks before 25 December. Whatever your preference, there is a wide, wide scope for bringing festive cheer to the hearth.

Bring out the Christmas tree decorations and lights and have fun decorating the tree. You might decide to make your own decorations, both edible and decorative. If you have children, decorating the tree brings enormous pleasure and the chance to make things for it is an exciting one. Edible fancies are, of course, especially tempting so ensure you have a few ideas for things to make.

Make a wreath for the front door to be hung from a length of twine, raffia or ribbon.

Hang up your Christmas cards.

TWO DAYS TO GO

Shopping

Buy your fresh fruit and vegetables now, but get out of the house early, before the shelves in the supermarkets start to become too empty. At home, store them somewhere cool, but frost-free. Keep potatoes in a darkened place, in a black poythene bag if necessary, or they will turn green. If your refrigerator is packed with other foods, a garage is the ideal storage place, but watch out for heavy frosts which might penetrate and affect delicate items like lettuces or brussel sprouts. Also make sure they are suitably protected from nosy roving animals.

Especially Christmassy items that should be purchased now are satsumas and delicious cheeses like Stilton. Other things you will need to think about are:

cream
fresh bread
fresh fruit juices
fruit
milk
sausages
vegetables

When you are buying your vegetables, plan for approximately 125 g (4 oz) per person for each meal.

If you have ordered turkey/game or other meat, don't forget to pick it up and then keep it in as cool a place as possible.

Cooking

If you have frozen turkey/game or other joint of meat, remove it from the freezer and keep somewhere cool while it thaws.

Check on the length of time you will need to cook the meat for so that you know how far in advance you will need to make the stuffing.

A detailed countdown for preparing the Christmas meal is given on page 66.

Decorating

Make your floral table centrepiece and any other arrangements. If you are using oasis, remember to soak it in advance of making the arrangement.

If your dining table is in a separate room that won't be disturbed before Christmas Day, consider laying it now. If not today, at least do it on Christmas Eve so that you can then forget about it.

HEATING AND SERVING FOOD

- Before serving hot dishes, make sure they are thoroughly cooked first.
- Don't keep food hot for more than an hour before people eat
- If you have food that can dry out, like sliced meat, cover it up with foil, cling film or a clean teacloth.
- Don't cover roast potatoes so that they remain crisp and dry.
- Casseroles retain their heat very well, as do root vegetables. But it is harder to keep leaf spinach or cabbage warm.
- Reheat cooked-chilled foods thoroughly before putting them on a hot tray or trolley.

Christmas crafts

Decorating
the
House

From welcoming wreaths to elaborate garlands, Christmas is a wonderful time to be creative and try out new decorating ideas for the home. The results are always rewarding and it's fun to get the whole family involved too – children love helping out and they will enjoy making their own decorations.

There are several projects to choose from in this chapter, from a simple advent calendar to a papier-mâché bowl. You'll find a project for everyone to enjoy, whatever their age and ability.

A COLOURFUL DISPLAY

Red, gold and green are traditional Christmas colours – and it's no wonder when you see how wonderfully rich they look. Ideal colours for decorations, they also give a warm glow to the home during the cold winter months. But of course you can choose any colours you like for your decorations – warm orange, glittering silver, rich purple and sparkling turquoise can also look stunning. For the best effect, decide on a colour scheme first, then follow it through, from the tree decorations to the mantelpiece and table setting, making sure everything works well together.

Glowing Greenery

Fresh evergreens, such as holly, ivy, mistletoe, pine and spruce are perfect for bringing glowing colour and a fresh scent to a room. Combined with soft candlelight, bowls of gleaming fruit and baskets of nuts and cones, evergreen foliage can transform an ordinary room into a scene of festive splendour. The simple idea of draping holly over pictures and mirrors, or attaching ivy along a mantelpiece instantly creates a seasonal feel. Spray some of the leaves with gold or silver paint to add a touch of shimmer.

Decorative Fruit

All manner of everyday produce can provide inspiration for home-made decorations – and often you do not need to look any further than your local supermarket! Citrus fruit has great potential for easy decorations. For example, fresh oranges add great colour to a display, and they have a delicious scent when studded with cloves. For extra sparkle rub the oranges with gilt wax, available from craft shops, then mix with plain oranges tied with wide organza ribbon. You can use this display throughout the house – from the hall console to the dinner table – and it will look and smell wonderful until the end of the holiday period.

This colourful festive display of fresh oranges combined with cloves and organza ribbon is simple to put together and will continue to look wonderful throughout the Christmas holiday.

Special Effects

One of the most dramatic ways to transform a room is to create an eye-catching display on a mantelpiece, table top or shelf. Candles are perfect for this purpose. They always look festive and for added sparkle simply place a nightlight in a small jam jar, wrap round some organza fabric and tie at the neck with gold cord. It's important to use a transparent fabric so you can actually see the flame – voile or muslin are both good alternatives to organza. Remember never to leave candles unattended.To make a simple yet effective natural-looking garland, string raffia underneath a mantelpiece, attaching it with tape or Blue-Tack, then tie on baby fir cones, small squares of frayed hessian with gold ribbon sewn or glued on, little pieces of bark and shells. To hang the shells, you will need to drill holes through them – this is a fairly easy task, just use a bradawl, but take care not to break the shell. Look out for other lightweight decorations to hang from the raffia – nut shells, leaves or dried flowers are a few ideas. As a finishing touch, try spraying parts of the garland gold to add a little sparkle. A window can also be dressed up to create a festive focal point. Baubles hanging from the recess are easily pinned up with drawing pins. Choose colours to complement the rest of the room. Candles, foliage, nuts and fruit displayed along the window sill offers instant atmosphere and warmth both inside and outside the house.

With a few simple decorations, a window recess or a mantelpiece can be turned into an eye-catching focal point.

Season's Greetings

An informal display of Christmas cards around a mirror instantly adds colour and seasonal atmosphere to a room.

Christmas cards come in an array of nostalgic and pretty designs, and are an obvious way of adding a seasonal feel to the house. To decorate a wall, fasten cards to lengths of ribbon with pins and then simply attach the ribbon with a drawing pin under a picture rail or coving. For a neat finish, add a rosette at the top. Alternatively, drape lengths of ribbon with cards attached over a door frame or display a selection of your favourite Christmas cards haphazardly around a mirror, to create a special feature in the hall or above a fireplace.

ROSETTES

Rosettes look pretty displayed on a Christmas tree, attached to a special gift or even as a finishing touch to a show of seasonal greeting cards pinned to lengths of ribbon. They are easy to make, but wire-edge ribbon is essential as it allows you to puff up the loops with the ribbon remaining in the arranged position. If you are unable to buy florist's wire, try using thin string or cotton.

YOU WILL NEED:

Wire-edge ribbon

Scissors

Florist's wire

■ Fold a length of ribbon in a zigzag pattern to create eight folds, allowing approximately 15 cm (6 inches) for each fold of ribbon (the length will depend on the size of rosette you wish to make). Then secure in the centre with florist's wire, leaving four loops each side.

■ Puff up the loops of ribbon to create a well-proportioned rosette.

A glorious rosette makes a stylish finishing touch to a show of seasonal cards.

UNUSUAL ADVENT CALENDAR

Advent is often forgotten in the build up to Christmas, but the much loved calendar is a must for most children. This very different version spirals its way to the top with the help of a shop-bought spiral twig base, spray paint, a silver marker pen and some foliage and it also proves how wooden pegs and greeting cards can be put to unconventional use! It is often unlikely items which turn out to be really useful when making your own decorations.

PAPIER-MÂCHÉ BOWL

You may find papier-mâché a time consuming hobby, but when you see the end result it is well worth the wait. This papier-mâché bowl makes an excellent Christmas gift, or a lovely decorative container. Fill the bowl with baubles for a festive display, or use for pot pourri or even pomanders with trailing ribbon as a special decoration for the dinner or coffee table. To make the filigree baubles shown in the picture, twist wire around a selection of coloured buttons to create a ball shape, then apply a couple of coats of Hilton's button polish.

YOU WILL NEED:

Mould (bowl or balloon)

Petroleum jelly

Shredded newspaper

PVA solution/Berol Marvin Medium

Small paint brush

Silver foil

Varnish/Hilton's button polish

■ Select a bowl or balloon and use as a mould for your papier-mâché bowl.

■ Cover the mould with petroleum jelly to avoid any paper sticking to the surface.

■ Apply a layer of shredded newspaper, then coat with a layer of dilute PVA water solution.

■ Allow to dry, then repeat the layering process until the required thickness is achieved – you will need approximately five to six layers.

■ Remove the papier-mâché bowl from the mould, paint on another layer of PVA solution and cover with a sheet of silver foil.

■ Varnish with Hilton's button polish for a distressed effect.

WREATHS AND GARLANDS

Although used for various occasions all year round, wreaths and garlands are a most common sight at Christmas time. A front door hung with a festive wreath, creates a very special entrance for visitors and gives an instant welcome. Inside, an elegantly draped garland around a window, mantelpiece or mirror can provide a focal point to the Christmas decorations in any room.

Both wreaths and garlands come in many different guises from the elegantly simple to the lavishly elaborate. There are no hard and fast rules when decorating a wreath or garland; you can really let your imagination run riot. In the mayhem of Christmas preparations there is not always time to create a wreath or garland from scratch, but don't worry because it is possible to buy twig wreath bases and fake fir garlands. As they are becoming increasingly popular, a good selection can be found ready made in most department stores and garden centres.

Don't feel restricted, however, to just those wreaths and garlands that you can buy in the shops. A basic wreath base or garland can easily be dressed up by adding a coloured ribbon or bow, some favourite Christmas decorations or perhaps bags of chocolate coins. Small gifts can be wrapped in tiny boxes covered in brightly coloured paper and attached to a wreath or garland using florist's wire. A wreath or garland could even be turned into an extravagant advent calendar by adding twenty-four miniature parcels and numbering each one for the days leading up to Christmas.

Fresh and dried flowers both make an equally stunning centrepiece when incorporated into a wreath or garland. Dried roses or bunches of lavender have the added bonus of smelling sweet as well as looking good, whilst fiery red dried chillies provide an unusual decorative touch. The cool, classic beauty of winter white roses set off by mistletoe and holly never fails to look stunning. When using fresh flowers and foliage, however, remember to use an oasis base and keep it moist.

FAKE-FIR GARLAND

Whether you decide to decorate the mantelpiece, window sill or a bare wall, garlands are always useful as a base for a decorative feature. First decide on a theme for your garland. You can use fresh fruit which will last for up to a couple of weeks, lengths of ribbon, fake berries, clusters of dried flowers and tree decorations. In fact, wherever you turn you are certain to find something to make good use of! Here small bunches of dried lavender and sweets, wrapped in a selection of sumptuous fabrics, adorn the garland. Wide ribbon or long strips of fabric always work well as a background cover.

It is very important to make sure everything is tied on securely, especially if you decide to use fresh fruit, which can be quite heavy. If you only have a few decorations to attach, make sure they appear evenly spaced out. Remember, too, that garlands look quite different when hanging up as opposed to lying flat.

YOU WILL NEED:
Fake-fir garland
Wire-edge ribbon
Dried lavender
Raffia
Scissors
Fabric
Pinking shears (optional)
Florist's wire
Cord
Small sweets

■ The amount of decorations needed depends on the length of the garland, but as a guide 10-15 items per metre should be enough.

■ Wrap wire-edge ribbon around the garland by twisting it around from one end to the other, making sure it is secure in both places. This adds good background colour.

■ Tie small bunches of dried lavender and attach with lengths of raffia.

■ Cut square pieces of fabric measuring about 25 cm (10 inches) square, and pink the edges with pinking shears, if using.

■ To make a fabric bag, place sweets in the middle of the material, tie with cord and attach the bag with florist's wire or raffia.

TRADITIONAL GARLAND

This dramatic arrangement looks stylish and is very easy to make. It is particularly well suited as the focus for a mantelpiece, but if you do not have a fireplace it would also look glorious on a window ledge, side-table or even a radiator cover. It could also be used as a centrepiece for a dining table, or as a decoration for a Christmas buffet. To create a stunning display put ivy, pine, oranges, lemons, spices and candles to good use. As long as you keep the oasis moist, the arrangement should last for a couple of weeks.

If you find it difficult to locate some of the items listed here, simply substitute other foliage of your choice. And, as an alternative to fruit, why not try using baubles or other Christmas tree decorations.

YOU WILL NEED:

Oasis

15 x 82 cm (6 x 33 inch) window-box tray

Terracotta flowerpots

Chicken wire

Florist's tape

Blue pine

Candles

Moss

Ivy

Florist's wire

Oranges

Lemons

Fir cones

Nuts

Cinnamon sticks

Ribbon

Variegated and berried holly

■ Place wet oasis on a window-box tray, then sink two terracotta flowerpots into this. Wrap chicken wire around the oasis, and secure to the tray with florist's tape.

■ Push blue pine into the oasis, cutting lengths about 30.5 cm (12 inches) long for the sides and 15-20.5 cm (6-8 inches) for the back, middle and front. Place candles in the flowerpots and keep them upright with clumps of moss.

■ Cut the ivy into 25 cm (10 inch) lengths and push into the wet oasis, evenly distributed between the blue pine. Cut some more ivy into longer lengths and push in around the centre and corners so that it can trail.

■ Push 30.5 cm (12 inch) pieces of florist's wire through the base of the fruit and twist. Attach more wire to the base of the fir cones and nuts and twist a few together. Tie bundles of cinnamon sticks with ribbon – choose a colour to match your decor – and twist wire around the back of the ribbon.

■ Add variegated and berried holly, distributing it evenly, then push in groups of the wired cones and nuts.

■ Push in groups of fruit, then complete the festive effect by adding the bundles of cinnamon sticks with their coloured ribbons.

HEART WREATH

Whether you choose fresh, dried or silk flowers, this charming heart wreath would look lovely anywhere in the house – from the front door to the chimney-breast. As a special treat for Christmas Day fresh flowers would look particularly glorious, although they obviously need to be arranged at the last moment. Alternatively, place oasis in tiny tin buckets and add a selection of fresh flowers, foliage and berries.

YOU WILL NEED:

Wire

Twigs

Fake berries

Raffia

Ribbon

Posies of fresh roses or silk flowers

Foliage

■ Bend several strands of wire into a heart shape.

■ Cover the heart shape with small bundles of twigs.

■ Add fake berries tied on with raffia or ribbon.

■ Wire small posies of fresh roses with some foliage and tie them on with ribbon. As an alternative to fresh flowers (which will obviously only last for a few hours without water) use dried or silk flowers.

TWIG WREATH

To make a special decoration for the front door, you can choose from an extensive collection of twig and fake evergreen wreaths. For this wreath, mosaic mirror decorations and gold-painted fir cones were used, but you can also try clusters of beads or look out for miniature Christmas tree decorations.

YOU WILL NEED:

Ready-made twig wreath

Scissors

Ribbon

Fir cones

Gold spray paint

Florist's wire

Tree decorations

Raffia

■ Twist ribbon around the wreath and tie a bow or rosette at the top.

■ Spray fir cones gold. When dry, take a small piece of florist's wire, secure around the base of the fir cone and attach to the wreath.

■ Thread tree decorations onto a long piece of raffia and twist around the wreath.

Christmas Trees

The tradition of decorating a tree for Christmas is thought to have started in Germany, and by the middle of the seventeenth century it had become customary throughout that country to adorn small fir trees with candles and fruit at Christmas time. The tree with its glorious decorations was introduced to Britian in the nineteenth century by Prince Albert and Queen Victoria. During this period people were encouraged to decorate a tree for the Christmas season – a custom which has been growing in popularity ever since. Today a traditional fir tree remains one of the most charming and prettiest of decorations to adorn the house at Christmas time and is certainly treasured by everyone young at heart!

THE TREE

A beautifully decorated Christmas tree is one of the happiest sights in December. It signals the beginning of the holiday season and, along with turkey and mince pies, is an essential element of the festivities. The Norway spruce has tended to be the favourite Christmas tree in Britain. In recent years, however, this has begun to change as other varieties have been found to hold their needles for longer. This may be an important consideration if you have pets or small children, so if you wish to buy a tree with good needle retention look out for Scots pine, Lodgepole pine, Noble fir and Nordmann fir or any tree that has been sprayed to minimise needle-drop.

Making the Most of Your Tree

Traditionally the tree should not be put up until Christmas Eve and then removed again by Twelfth Night (6 January), but in recent years the decorating of the tree has crept forward to much earlier in the month. This extended period inside the home can cause problems for the tree as central heating causes it to dry out so that by Christmas Day it can look past its best. To avoid these problems always buy a fresh tree that hasn't already started to dry out. The easiest way to check for freshness before buying a tree is to hold a branch snugly between your thumb and forefinger several inches from the end, then pull your hand towards the end. The branch should not lose many needles. If it does, the tree is already drying out and you should choose another.

Most Christmas trees are sold as cut trees, although it is possible to buy one with its roots still intact. Trees with bare roots have simply been pulled up rather than cut. They tend to be smaller in size and, if potted in moist earth, they may survive if planted out. Root-balled trees have been carefully dug up and the roots and earth have been wrapped in sacking. After removing the sacking the tree should be potted in moist earth, and is likely to survive if planted out. Potted trees have been dug up with their roots and then potted afterwards. If the tree does not look fresh, the roots may have dried out before potting took place. Container grown trees are usually quite small, and have actually been grown in their pots, so should survive from one Christmas to the next, although they may need repotting into a larger container to allow better growth.

Artificial trees have also increased in popularity and authenticity over recent years. Things have moved on from the garish tinsel wrapped branches, and there are now some very realistic looking fake fir trees available. The benefit of an artificial tree is that it will last year on year, although the initial cost of buying the tree can be quite high, and that you won't suffer the problem of dropping needles. One of the drawbacks, however, is that you will miss out on the delightful scent of pine that you can only get from a real fir tree.

All cut trees need a surprising amount of water, which will allow them to stay fresh for longer. Keeping up the moisture content of the tree also reduces the risk of fire hazard, so it is a good idea to place a cut tree in a water-holding container throughout the Christmas period. When you get your tree home leave it outside with a damp towel wrapped around the butt until you are ready to move it indoors then, just before you put up the tree, make a straight, half-inch cut across the base of the trunk to remove the layer of sap that forms and prevents the absorption of water. After trimming the trunk, get the tree into a stand

right away, and give it some water. If more than a few hours go by, a new layer of sap can develop, and you'll need to cut the trunk again.

Before you can put the tree into a stand, however, you need to get it through the house to the spot you have chosen for it. Don't put it near a source of heat or ventilation – all trees last longer if kept away from direct heat. Transporting even a fresh, healthy tree through a house often means leaving a trail of pine needles behind you. Contain the mess by wrapping the tree in an old sheet.

Decorating Your Tree

Christmas tree lights and garlands come in many varieties, from the simple to the highly elaborate; again, it is a matter of personal choice. When decorating a tree, however, always put up any lights and garlands first, and then add the ornaments. To arrange the lights evenly, wind the wire around the tree form the bottom upwards. Always fit a 3 amp fuse to the plug for Christmas lights, and make sure they are unplugged before tightening or replacing bulbs. If you have any queries or problems, always consult a professional electrician.

Ornaments often become family heirlooms, being passed from one generation to the next. To keep them from falling and breaking, attach them to the tree with lengths of floral wire instead of sharp hooks or flimsy thread. Cut green florist's wire into 10–15 cm (4–6 in) lengths. Loop one end through the ornament, and twist it tight. Twist the other end directly around a tree branch a few times, anchoring it between needles. When decorating the tree it is a good idea to wear protective gloves and a long-sleeved shirt as you work – the needles are sharper then you think.

Although candles on a tree can look very pretty, they are extremely hazardous. If you are determined to use them, always take the following precautions. Spray the foliage with a fire-retardant spray before decorating; make sure the candles are fixed firmly upright and in a position where they cannot burn a branch; never leave the candles burning unattended; check the tree is well away from curtains etc, and keep a fire extinguisher or bucket of water nearby just in case.

Dismantling Your Tree

Eventually you will have to reverse the whole process and take down the tree. As you start to work, the tree will lose needles, so put a sheet on the floor to catch them. Detach the ornaments from the branches and wrap each one individually in tissue paper – preferably acid-free. Return the ornaments to the boxes they came in; it's a good idea to keep them as they are, of course, a perfect fit. If you don't have the original boxes pack the ornaments in sturdy containers with cardboard dividers inside with tissue paper. Don't forget to label the boxes so the next year you can easily find what you are looking for. When you take down the lights, wind each strand into a neat bundle, and place each one in a plastic bag to stop them getting tangled. When removing the tree, take it out the way it was brought in – wrapped in a sheet to contain the needles. Sweep up as many needles as you can, then vacuum the remaining dirt; needles aren't good for your vacuum cleaner. And remember, Christmas trees can be recycled.

TREE DECORATIONS

The Christmas tree is a much-loved symbol of the festive season and for most of us it is also an essential part of the Christmas decorations. There is immense pleasure and satisfaction in the ritual of decking out the family tree, and now that decorations have become far more innovative and interesting, it seems to be easier to create a special and individual look.

The decorations you choose for the tree can be as unique as you wish. Ready-made decorations are available in abundance from specialist gift shops, department stores and garden centres up and down the country. The choice is almost endless, ranging from delicate glass baubles and twinkling silver tinsel to traditional wooden hanging shapes.

Whether you buy your decorations or wish to make your own, the most important advice to follow is to concentrate on a theme. Decide on a style and colourway and then stick to it. This is by far the easiest way to create a co-ordinated and harmonious looking Christmas tree. Themes can be anything from warm shades of red and green, rich medieval designs, Highland tartan, opulent jewel-like colours, edible biscuits and fruits, nostalgic, novelty, or even the simple New England style. Use magazines and books as a source of inspiration and always look out for good ideas in local shops, home accessory stores and even nature itself, particularly if you would like a natural theme.

You can also create a unique effect by making your own decorations.

Home-made Baubles

Making your own baubles is fun. It's also a great way to create an individual and novel look for your Christmas tree. The quickest and simplest idea is to wrap a small piece of fabric around a polystyrene ball and simply secure with ribbon. Look out for seasonal fabrics, such as the popular star motif, in dress fabric departments at a local store. Or try your hand at making your own design by stencilling inexpensive calico fabric.

For a touch of luxury — and an eye-catching display – it is well worth using sumptuous chenille yarn with gold trimmings. Raffia can also be used in the same way as chenille, but you may find it is rather slippery to handle and therefore more difficult to keep in place.

Polystyrene balls look just as good painted and decorated with anything from buttons to dried beans – use glue for sticking the decorations in place. Apples and oranges look festive decorated with beads, cord and raffia. If they seem to be too heavy for the Christmas tree, try hanging the decorations in a window or attach to garlands and wreaths. Other fruits such as limes and lemons also look stunning.

Edible Decorations

In Victorian days Christmas trees were adorned with edible decorations and there is no reason why you shouldn't continue this charming tradition. Use the recipe for Gingerbread Tree Decorations on page 182 to create seasonal shapes, such as bells, Christmas trees and gingerbread men. Alternatively, make or buy marzipan fruit, thread with loops of narrow gold braid and decorate with bows of gold or tartan ribbon.

This pretty bauble is made by simply wrapping chenille yarn around a polystyrene or oasis ball, then finishing with gold braid and upholstery tacks.

SPRAYED BAUBLES

Spray paint is a quick and easy way of coating the ball, and dried beans, available from any food shop, produce an interesting effect. Look out for other edible items to use instead of the beans.

YOU WILL NEED:
Spray paint
Polystyrene ball
Cord
Beads (optional)
Glue
Dried beans

■ Spray the polystyrene ball and allow it to dry.

■ Decorate with cord and tie a loop at the top. Thread beads through the cord, if using.

■ Glue on the dried beans.

FRUIT BAUBLES

Adorn the tree with fresh fruit to add a splash of vibrant colour. As fresh fruit baubles are quite heavy they may be better suited to hang on an artificial tree because the branches are stronger and will not bend so easily. Alternatively, use fresh fruit baubles to decorate a fake fir garland or display in a window. You may find they look better hanging at different levels.

YOU WILL NEED:
Apples
Oranges or clementines
Raffia or cord
Beads

■ Neatly wind raffia or cord around your chosen piece of fruit, as if you are tying a ribbon around a parcel. To secure, tie a knot.

■ Tie a loop at the top and thread beads through the raffia.

■ As an extra decoration tie another piece of raffia to the base and thread more beads through.

■ Tie a knot and fray the remaining raffia.

CARDBOARD STARS

Cardboard stars look particularly good when the ridges are highlighted with gold paint. The corrugated texture looks most effective when displayed against shapes made from smoother materials.

YOU WILL NEED:

Pencil

Tracing paper

Scissors

Corrugated card

Spray paint

Gold paint

Small paint brush

Raffia or ribbon

■ Draw an eight-pointed star shape and trace onto a piece of corrugated card.

■ To make stars of various sizes, simply enlarge the tracing on a photocopier.

■ Use spray paint to colour the surface.

■ Highlight the cardboard ridges with gold paint.

■ When dry, make a small hole and thread with raffia or ribbon to make a loop.

YOU WILL NEED:

Twig tree with wooden stand

Starfish

Scallop shells

Conch shells

Gold, copper, cream and red spray paints

Raffia

Rope

SEA TREASURE TREE

If you feel like a change from the traditional look, this unusual 'twig' tree will inspire you. To decorate the tree, we have used seashore finds and painted them in classic red and gold colours – you can vary the paints as you like, to match your own colour scheme. As an extra effect, we have painted the starfish red and then sponged them with gold.

■ Spray the starfish and shells with the spray paints and allow to dry.

■ Using raffia, tie the scallop shells onto a long piece of rope and drape around the tree.

■ Arrange the remaining decorations on the tree, by gently pushing between the twigs.

The Christmas Table

As family and friends gather for the Christmas festivities, much of the day will be spent enjoying a traditional meal around the dining table. Discover how you can simply add a few extra touches to your existing china to enjoy a perfect setting for Christmas Day lunch and make every meal a special visual treat throughout the festive season.

CREATING THE LOOK

To create an impressive and successful table setting for Christmas it is necessary to decide on a colour theme first. Take your china and glassware as a starting point, and then build up a scheme around your crockery using napkins, candles, foliage, decorations and flowers to complement the look. If your china is white, for instance, you can opt for almost any colour combination – try partnering white with warm shades of copper, deep red, antique gold, purple and bright orange for a stunning effect. Or if blue is the predominant colour, try experimenting with silver, green and touches of ochre. But to achieve an harmonious look, it is advisable to work around at least one of the colours which appears in the china pattern.

Whether you choose rich opulent shades or splashes of sophisticated gold, it is a good idea to look at the room as a whole. The two dining rooms pictured here and on the previous page look very different, but both settings have similar elements, such as elegant white china with a gold rim and clear glasses with touches of gold decoration.

If your dining room is decorated in strong colours, then this allows you to carry on using the same tones for the dining table without any major problems. A neutral decor on the other hand, tends to lend itself to a cleaner and calmer look. In the case of the latter, if you already have a traditional white damask tablecloth, then make good use of it and add colour elsewhere.

White and Gold

In the picture opposite, the white and gold combination has been complemented with fresh foliage and a few purple flowers; we used anemones and potted winter pansies. The gold theme continues with candles in unusual pineapple and pear shapes which have been carefully arranged on a platter in the middle of the table. White damask napkins receive an easy-to-copy napkin ring treatment – simply twist gold wire-edge ribbon into a rope and knot the ends around the napkin. And finally fresh floral garlands have been placed round the bottom of the wine glasses. To make these, wind a small piece of ivy into a circle, then wire on flower heads in colours to suit your theme. Make sure you allow enough space to be able to remove the wine glass without difficulty! As the flowers are fresh, this decoration needs to be made at the last minute. However, dried or even silk flowers can look just as effective. They will obviously last longer, when handled with care, and can also be made in advance. For many this is a great help during the hectic build up to Christmas.

Red and Gold

In the other dining room pictured on page 36-37, deep red painted walls and an ornate ceiling allows a richer colour scheme to work well for the table setting. The combination of red and purple silk dupion brings the base colour to the table, while the jade and gold trim

napkins add an element of surprise to the overall colour theme. Candles give a warm and cosy feel to the room and look welcoming both on the table and mantelpiece. Instead of using flowers for the centre of the table, a glass bowl on a metal stand is filled with gold chocolate coins (available from most supermarkets) and purple glass Christmas tree baubles. It is a simple decoration, but in this case an elaborate floral arrangement is not necessary as it would detract from the rest of the table setting, which appears wonderfully rich and opulent to the eye. As an alternative to chocolate coins and baubles, try fresh fruit with a sprinkling of icing sugar for a magical frosted effect. Other finishing touches shown here include name tags tied onto gilt pears, beautifully wrapped individual gifts and napkins decorated with gold cord and tassels. These simple details help to give a well-harmonised look.

Napkins are perfect for introducing a splash of colour to a table setting.

A beautifully wrapped gift arranged at a place setting enhances the colour scheme and makes an interesting alternative to a cracker.

DECORATIVE DETAILS

Once you have decided on a colour theme, you can start to think about the decorative details that will help to set the mood of the table setting.

Table-top Tips

Deciding on how to cover the table is a good starting point. If you do not have a large enough tablecloth it is worth considering buying either calico or paper to cover the table, instead of investing in a new cloth which may not be needed again for quite some time.

Calico fabric provides a neutral cream background and you will find it is very easy to stencil. A star motif is of course very seasonal, but today a wide range of stencil designs are available. Choose one which will enhance your theme – maybe an ivy leaf trail, a simple heart motif, angels, cherubs or even a tudor rose. To make matching calico napkins, cut out 50 cm (20 inch) square pieces of cloth, turn the edges and stitch down, then stencil your chosen design in each corner.

Using a large cotton bed sheet is also a good alternative to a new tablecloth, and usually considerably less expensive. Instead of stencilling, have a go at drawing your own designs with a felt tip pen. If you find this too daunting, try using a stencil motif as a guide and fill in the shape by scribbling – in one direction only – with a felt tip pen. Choose a colour to suit your theme. It is quicker and just a little different to the usual paint brush effect. To highlight the design, simply use plain paper napkins that tie in with the colours of the pattern.

If you have a lovely wooden table-top you may want to use table mats only. Again, you can always make your own mats from plain, thick fabric and stencil on a pattern to enhance the theme of the table setting. For an attractive finish, try using material that can be frayed at the edges. Another idea for place mats is to weave together different coloured ribbons (see page 46), or you can create simple, colourful mats in a matter of minutes by cutting shapes from felt or from metallic coloured thin card. If the table top is heat resistant, you could opt for a natural look and create mats from brown paper – just stamp on a design of your choice. Enhance the natural feel by using raffia to decorate crackers for the table. Shop-bought crackers with a plain matt finish could also be stamped or stencilled with your chosen design to continue the theme.

The star shapes of the candle holders reflect the pattern on the tablecloth to give an overall theme to the table setting.

Special Touches

Adding a few simple finishing touches to place settings can make all the difference to the overall effect of the table, turning a Christmas meal into a memorable event.

A small gift placed at each setting is very much in the Christmas spirit and adds a personal touch. Individual foil-wrapped chocolates make perfect gifts, as do small boxes of Turkish delight or glacé fruit. Sugared almonds gathered up in coloured cellophane or net and tied with ribbon look attractive, while home-made fudge, placed inside small ready-made decorative bags with string handles, will be greeted with delight.

A quick and easy way to dress up wine glasses is to tie a ribbon bow around each stem – wire-edge, fine gold ribbon looks very effective used in this way. For a stylish touch, write out the menu using a gold marker pen and place it in a gilt picture frame to stand on the table.

The gold finishing touches on this delicate table setting focus on stars and shells for a pretty effect.

Name Cards

A seating plan is advisable and helpful whether you are hosting a formal dinner party or just a simple gathering for family and friends. Traditional place cards and holders have become very popular – glass star holders are particularly seasonal – but you can also make your own tags for an individual look. If you want to avoid cluttering the table, try cutting out stars from gold card and tying them to the chair backs with some striking gold cord or wrapping ribbon. To make free-standing cards look more seasonal, try cutting coloured card into Christmas tree shapes, or Christmas pudding-shaped cards are fun for a change. Use gold or silver pens to write the names on the cards.

FRUIT TAGS

For a name tag with a difference, try this simple idea with fruit. It's also an excellent way of adding an element of gold to the table. You can substitute apples for the pears if you wish.

YOU WILL NEED

Wax gilt

Firm pears, with stems

Red card

Scissors

Hole punch

Gold pen

Gold ribbon

■ First rub the pears with wax gilt, to cover the fruit evenly. Cut out name tags from the red card and use the gold pen to write on the names.

■ Punch a hole in one corner of each card and tie to the stem of the fruit with gold ribbon.

Napkin Rings

Whether you decide to use paper or fabric napkins, a napkin ring is useful and adds a simple decorative finishing touch to your table setting. The easiest solution for a home-made napkin ring is to tie ribbon around the napkin in a bow, then to simply add some winter foliage for decoration. A glossy leaf can also double up as a name tag. For a festive feel use a gold or silver marker pen to write the names of your guests.

Another simple idea is to twist wire-edge ribbon into a rope and then knot the ends to make a circular shape. Ribbon with wire along each edge is a little more expensive, but is very easy to handle and takes the worry out of making pretty bows and rosettes too!

Rings and Things

Wooden curtain rings can also come in useful as napkin rings or even for placing around the cutlery at each table setting. Arranged on the dinner plate, this idea can look quite fun. Remove the metal eye from the curtain hook, then either paint the ring or wrap ribbon around it. If using ribbon, make sure you leave two loose ends for the bow, or simply tie a knot and cut a v-shape at each loose end.

You can also make napkin rings from cardboard or even corrugated card. This is available in a selection of colours, so you can choose one to suit your colour scheme. For fun, make the napkin ring extra special by adding a colourful candy stick and holding them together with ribbon. This is guaranteed to go down well if children are sitting down at the dinner table!

But why not experiment with your own ideas for unusual napkin treatments. Gold tassels, cord, shells, cinnamon sticks, foliage and gold painted fir cones all look pretty.

A candy stick is attached to a simple corrugated card napkin ring holder to add a touch of fun to a place setting, while a plain wooden curtain ring is encased in ribbon to create an attractive holder for cutlery.

Crackers

Crackers are always popular at Christmas. Filled with an amazing selection of hats, jokes and gimmicky presents, they add a fun note to the dining table. Today the choice is vast with crackers to suit almost every setting, as designs range from nostalgic and traditional to novelty and contemporary. But these ready-made crackers often turn out to be an expensive purchase. Filling your own crackers with personal gifts is a cheaper and increasingly more popular choice, and empty crackers are now widely available from the shops. Alternatively, look out for plain crackers which are quick and easy to jazz up with wide ribbon, strips of pretty fabric along the edges, beads, fake berries or even fresh foliage.

HOME-MADE CRACKERS

If time allows, why not have a go at making your own personalised crackers for your guests. Apart from looking pretty, home-made crackers also mean that each guest is more likely to receive a suitable gift! Look out for presents which are small enough to fit into the cracker or simply fill with chocolates and other sweets. An empty loo-roll is the ideal size for the cardboard tube, and for the decorations, use shiny paper, beads, sequins, pieces of fabric – whatever you have to hand.

YOU WILL NEED:
Thin, soft paper
Cardboard tube
Scissors
Small gifts
Cracker snapper (optional)
Paper glue
Raffia, ribbon or string
Pinking scissors
Decorations

■ Cut thin soft paper so that it is 10 cm (4 inches) longer than the tube.

■ Place the tube in the centre of the paper. Put the gift and snapper, if using, into the tube and wrap the paper around the tube to enclose. Glue the edge down.

■ Gather the excess paper at either end of the roll and tie quite tightly with raffia, ribbon or string.

■ Pink the edges, then glue on decorations.

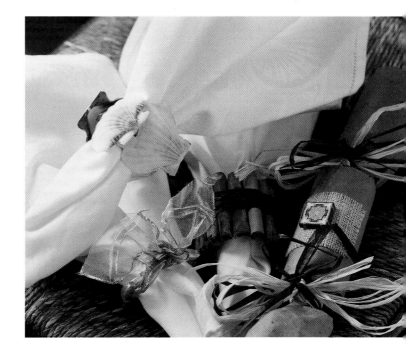

The decorations on the home-made cracker shown here combine purple colours with natural-looking raffia and hessian, to co-ordinate with a selection of home-made napkin holders.

WOVEN PLACE MAT

Make your own woven place mats from felt for a unique and fun table setting this Christmas. Remember to choose colours which will complement your china. You may still wish to use a tablecloth, so it is also necessary to consider its colour and pattern before you go out and buy the felt. As an alternative to felt, you could use strips of ribbons to weave the mat.

YOU WILL NEED:

Felt, in two contrasting colours

Sharp scissors

Pencil

Ruler

Fabric glue

Needle

Thread

Calico or lining fabric

■ Measure the plates you will be using and allow for an extra 8-10 cm (3-4 inches) on either side.

■ Cut strips of felt in each colour – the amount depends on the width of the strips you cut.

■ Lay all the cut pieces of one colour in vertical lines, then start weaving through the other colour strips in horizontal lines.

■ When you have finished, turn the ends over to one side and fasten with glue. Alternatively use a needle and thread.

■ For a neat finish stitch on a plain backing using calico or lining fabric.

A CENTREPIECE

To complete any table setting, you will need an eye-catching centrepiece. Tall floral arrangements may obstruct your view when talking to guests. A low table decoration is therefore ideal for any gathering, large or small, as it is easy to talk over. A simple bowl of fruit interspersed with foliage and Christmas baubles is quick to put together yet looks very attractive, while a candle arrangement adds a warm, subtle glow and imparts a pleasing shape to the setting.

Christmas Flowers

If you opt for a centrepiece of fresh flowers, it is worth deciding on your choice of container first. You can use terracotta plant pots, plates, bowls, sundae dishes, teapots and even fresh fruit to create a number of unusual floral arrangements. Choose containers which work well together and arrange them in groups of three or five depending on the size of your dining table. It also looks more interesting if you can vary the height and size of the containers.

Vases with a Difference

Using fruit or vegetables as a vase works very well, and can look colourful. Peppers are a particularly good choice as they come in wonderfully bright shades of red, orange, yellow and green. If you decide to use peppers, simply trim the stem and use that end as the base, making sure it is well balanced. Cut off the top of the pepper to form a container. You can either put oasis inside for the flowers or, if it is completely water-tight, just fill with water, then arrange your selection of flowers. Melons and pineapples also make stunning containers, with ivy and other trailing foliage cascading down the sides. Just scoop out the fruit (make sure you can use it in one of your recipes instead of throwing it away) and then fill with oasis or water as above.

Both large and small bowls can be filled with blooms floating in water. Glass containers usually look best, because they are transparent. Try adding a few floating candles for a glowing effect, and for extra colour and texture put glass nuggets, shells or pebbles in the bottom of the bowl. China bowls can also be used for floating blooms as long as they are shallow enough to allow you to see the contents.

Another idea for a low arrangement is to use a terracotta dish lined with moss as a base. Fill small flower pots with growing plants such as pansies or violets, even herbs or trailing ivy, and then arrange your selection of potted plants on the moss base. As a finishing touch fill any gaps with fir cones.

Candle Power

Candles instantly add atmosphere to a table setting and are perfect for creating a stunning centrepiece. Finding the right candles is surprisingly easy these days as the choice available is vast. Whether you want novelty shapes, church or beeswax candles, ornate gilt shapes, coloured nightlights, scented candles or simply a pair of classic tapered candles, you are sure to find something suitable. And, with the right container and a little imagination, creating a centrepiece can can be very simple.

Terracotta Transformed

Terracotta plant pots make wonderful containers for candles. Very inexpensive, they can be left plain if that suits your colour scheme and table setting. Alternatively they can be painted, covered with paper or fabric or left natural with a ribbon tied round for extra decoration. Place a chunky candle inside and surround with shells, pebbles or moss both for decoration and to hold it firmly in place.

Alternatively, line the pot with plastic, fill with oasis, then secure the candle in the middle and decorate with fresh flowers and foliage around the base of the candle. It is also fun to mix flowers with fruit such as apples, limes, lemons and oranges. Simply push a 30.5 cm (12 inch) piece of florist's wire through the base of the fruit and twist, then push the wire into the oasis as you would with the stems of the flowers. As an alternative to fresh flowers, dried lavender, roses and eucalyptus mixed with fir cones and cinnamon sticks also looks great for Christmas and obviously lasts a great deal longer!

Candles and Fruit

Fruit-shaped candles look decorative and can be used to great effect in an arrangement. A wooden seed box, transformed with a lick of paint, is a useful container for displaying 'fruit' candles. First line the box with plastic then fill with moss and arrange the candles on top.

Try interspersing the candles with real fruit – apples, clementines, limes and bunches of red grapes – to create a colourful display. An ivy garland adds a finishing touch to this arrangement.

Fresh fruits such as oranges, small pineapples, squashes and apples also make fun candle holders for nightlights or candles. First make sure the fruit stands up on its own. If not, simply slice off a small piece at the bottom to make a flat base. Using a spoon scoop out some of the fruit flesh, making a hole large enough to hold a nightlight. Decorate the edge around the candle by pushing cloves into the fruit. If you are using taller candles, line the gaps between the fruit and the candles with moss. This will secure the candle, keeping it in place while lit.

A wooden seed box receives a lick of paint and becomes an excellent container for this unusual selection of 'fruit' candles.

CANDLE WREATH

A ready-made, shop-bought twig wreath is an excellent base for a candle table decoration. This is ideal for large gatherings, as the arrangement is low enough for diners to talk over. Candle clips, which are usually seen on Christmas trees, are used for attaching the candles to the wreath. Simply clip the candles onto the twig base, and for extra decoration fill the centre with fruit and baubles.

Gifts

Gifts are a pleasure to give and delightful to receive, but are even more so when they come beautifully and imaginatively wrapped! A pile of presents tucked under the Christmas tree is a decoration in itself, and will look even better if a little time and careful thought has been put into the presentation. Even the smallest and least costly gift can look like a luxurious treat with a little help from trailing ribbon and pretty paper.

WRAPPING UP

Before you start on the task of wrapping all your gifts, you need to consider the different shapes and sizes of the items you intend to wrap. Also, you need to ask yourself who the gifts are for – a child, teenager, elderly relative, partner or friend, male or female? All these elements are important to remember and take into consideration before you go out and buy large amounts of paper and ribbon.

You can be as imaginative as you wish with the presentation of your gifts. In the run up to Christmas you will find inspiring ideas everywhere you look – in gift shops, magazines and books. The range of wrapping paper available today is extensive with stunning contemporary, humorous and traditional designs to choose from.

However, if you have some spare time why not have a go at creating your own motifs on plain paper. Brown parcel paper or even lining paper are both excellent choices for stamping, stencilling or drawing your own designs. For a natural look, in keeping with the colour of the paper, choose raffia instead of ribbon to tie up your parcel. And, if you decide to use string, complete the look with sealing wax to resemble a parcel of bygone days!

Stencilling with a difference – create an unusual stencil effect with a coloured felt-tip pen by scribbling in one direction , leaving small gaps so you can see the paper between the lines. It is quick and easy to cover a large sheet of paper and the end result looks great too.

Stencilling and Stamping

The idea of using a stamp to create designs is now becoming popular, and you will find stamps quicker and much easier to use than stencils. You can even make your own stamp using a large potato. Simply cut the potato in half, draw a motif on cardboard, making sure it is smaller than the potato itself, and use as a template. Place the template onto the cut potato, hold down firmly and draw around the motif with a felt tip pen. Carefully cut around the design with a knife to make a relief pattern. For stamping out the design, you can either use an ink pad or paint. The latter is best applied with a small roller.

However, if you choose a stencil design, have a go at filling in the shape with a felt tip pen instead of following the traditional method with brush and paint. For a successful result make sure you draw or scribble lines in one direction only, allowing the paper underneath to show through slightly.

Another alternative to stencilling is to make a template – choose a seasonal motif such as a star or tree, place it in position on the wrapping paper, and then spray paint around the design. Gold paint on a corrugated card background, for instance, adds extra sparkle and original appeal.

Little and Large

Unless a large gift comes packaged in a box (which is easy to wrap up in pretty paper) it can be almost impossible to cover – the paper usually isn't wide enough, it tears easily and the end result can often look in a sorry state. The best solution is to turn to calico or hessian fabric.

A sack is quick and easy to sew together along three seams, then you can simply tie it together with a large bow at the top. You can also decorate the fabric using stencils or stamps, which come in a wide range of designs suitable for both children and adults alike. Alternatively, cut out shapes from felt and then glue or stitch onto the sack. After the event, simply keep for another occasion or use as next year's Christmas stocking for the children.

For large parcels, make sure you choose a wide ribbon. Or, if you prefer raffia, use a fair-sized bundle for a full bow. Wrapping paper with a large pattern is well suited for big gifts. If you plan to decorate your own paper, even just one motif like a star or tree covering each side, would look attractive.

Small gifts are much easier to wrap, and therefore less awkward to handle. First, remember to choose wrapping paper with a scaled-down pattern repeat or even just plain paper in cheerful colours. Tissue paper is particularly good to use for smaller gifts. It comes in a wide range of beautiful colours from traditional red and green to bright pink and turquoise. There are several sheets of paper in each bundle, and although it is fairly transparent, one sheet will be enough for a small item. If you prefer using ribbon, make sure it is not too wide and thus in keeping with the size of the gift. Cord is an excellent substitute for ribbon, and comes in festive gold and silver too. Instead of tying a bow, fray the ends after knotting.

Tissue paper is perfect for wrapping small gifts. Here, a wonderful selection of brightly coloured tissue paper and gold cord has been used to wrap little gifts for friends, cleverly displayed in a plain glass bowl.

Useful Boxes

You may find it helpful to gather a few boxes for wrapping gifts which have awkward shapes. Shoe boxes are particularly useful, because they have a lid. You can easily cover the box and lid separately using either wrapping paper, remnants of wall paper or even swatches of fabric. A covered box can even be a present in itself – if you attach ribbon to the inside of the lid, the ribbon will not need to be removed when the box is opened.

DECORATIVE FINISHES

Whether the parcel is small or large, it is a good idea to add other decorations to create a very special and eye-catching package. It need not cost a great deal – a piece of holly or ivy from the garden for instance, would look wonderful attached to the bow. Clusters of fake berries also make perfect decorations. These are available from most shops selling Christmas decorations.

You can also make your own decorations by spray painting fir cones. Attach a piece of florist's wire to the base of the cone and then twist a bundle of three together.

Bundles of cinnamon sticks tied together with ribbon or small posies of dried flowers, also make excellent decorations for gifts. Secure to the gift with a small piece of florist's wire twisted around the ribbon. These decorations can be used as an alternative to the traditional bow, but combining the two would also look appealing – especially when decorating a larger gift.

Name Tags

Ready-made name tags are often uninspiring, so it is well worth making your own. Home-made name tags are quick and easy to create and add a special personal touch to your gift. One sheet of thin card, a pair of sharp scissors and a marker pen or felt tip pen is all you need. You can usually choose from a wide range of colours, or buy white card and decorate it yourself.

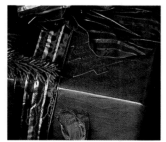

SHAPED NAME TAG

First find a suitable item or picture to use as a template – keep the design simple; a Christmas tree, moon, star or bell shape would be ideal. If you are using a picture, trace it onto stiff card to make the template. To cut out the name tag, place the template in position on card, draw around it using a pencil and then cut out the shape. If the pencil lines are still showing just rub them away for a neater look. As a finishing touch use gold or silver marker pens to write a personal message.

GREETING CARDS

Sending seasonal messages and greetings of good will is a familiar pastime during the build up to Christmas. In the shops, there are cards to suit any taste, but making your own selection of personalised cards for family and friends can be great fun and will be much appreciated by the recipient.

There are several materials which are suitable for making Christmas cards. Be creative and experiment with hessian and beads, raffia and cord, stencils and spray paint, dried flowers and feathers, to mention but a few. Even cuttings from newspapers and magazines put together as a collage can look glorious.

Another idea is to cut out tree and star shapes from felt and sew them onto craft paper with blanket stitching. Use buttons for extra decorations and for a neat finish, cover the back of the card with another piece of paper – either glue it on or stitch the two pieces together. Watercolour paper has a great texture and craft paper comes in several wonderful colours.

A HOME-MADE CHRISTMAS CARD

This simple yet striking card is easy to make and requires few items. You can also ring the changes by simply choosing a different colour scheme.

YOU WILL NEED:

Watercolour paper

Scissors

Hole punch

Raffia, ribbon, cord or string

Hessian

Glue

Beads or dried leaves

■ Cut a piece of watercolour paper into two equal-sized pieces, then tear to give a rough edge.

■ Punch holes on one side and tie hinges (loosely) using raffia, ribbon, cord or string.

■ Cut a small piece of hessian to cover part of the front page. Fray the edges and glue on.

■ Decorate the card with beads, raffia tied into a bow or dried leaves. Attach to the hessian with glue.

Christmas food

Easy
Christmas Eve Menu 1

On the night before Christmas, there's such a lot going on that the last thing you want to do is to spend time preparing a complicated meal for staying guests, particularly if you are planning a special lunch for the next day. Follow this quick-to-prepare menu to ensure that you are free to enjoy all the excitement of Christmas Eve and, at the same time, are able to produce a light, tasty meal that will be much appreciated by everyone.

In this menu, the soup takes a matter of minutes to prepare with the help of a food processor; use a carton of freshly squeezed orange juice to speed up the finishing time. For an instant accompaniment to the soup, we suggest flavouring ready-made Italian bread with herbs – a useful tip for spicing up quick meals. Salmon roasted in a mustard butter couldn't be easier to prepare and the saffron-flavoured potatoes are created by simply adding the spice to the cooking water. A fuss-free meal in minutes!

MENU FOR 6

Tomato, Pepper and Orange Soup
Hot Rosemary Ciabatta

Roast Salmon in Mustard Butter
Saffron Potatoes

Chilled Grapes and Vignotte

COUNTDOWN

To serve at 8pm
7pm Make the soup ready to reheat.
Take the cheese out of the refrigerator.

7.30pm Preheat the oven to 230°C (450°F) mark 8. Prepare the salmon and put in the oven to cook. Make the rosemary ciabatta and put in the oven to heat. Prepare the potatoes and put on to cook. Chill the grapes.

7.45pm Reheat the soup to a simmer.
Toss the salad leaves.

8pm Serve the soup. Cover the potatoes and salmon and keep warm.

Tomato, Pepper and Orange Soup

70 cals per serving

400 g (14 oz) can pimientos (red peppers), drained

few sprigs fresh rosemary or 5 ml (1 tsp) dried

10 ml (2 tsp) caster sugar

1 litre (1¾ pints) tomato juice

300 ml (10 fl oz) chicken stock

450 ml (15 fl oz) freshly squeezed orange juice

salt and pepper

orange slices and rosemary sprigs, to garnish

Hot Rosemary Ciabatta, to serve

1 In a food processor, blend together the pimientos, rosemary, sugar and half the tomato juice.

2 Sieve the mixture into a saucepan and stir in the stock with the orange juice, remaining tomato juice and salt and pepper.

3 Bring to the boil and simmer gently for about 10 minutes. Adjust the seasoning and serve, garnished with orange slices and rosemary sprigs.

Freezing: suitable, after simmering. Thaw overnight in the refrigerator, reheat and garnish.

Roast Salmon in Mustard Butter

560 cals per serving

1.1 kg (2½ lb) piece boned middle cut of salmon

175 g (6 oz) melted butter

45 ml (3 tbsp) wholegrain mustard

20 ml (4 tsp) dried dill weed

salt and pepper

275 g (10 oz) fresh spinach, rocket or mixed salad leaves

1 Open out the salmon like a book until almost flat by pressing along the backbone area. Place skin-side up in a shallow ovenproof dish just large enough to hold it.

2 Mix together the butter, mustard, dill and salt and pepper. Pour over the salmon. Cook at 230°C (450°F) mark 8 for about 20 minutes or until just tender.

3 Toss the salad leaves and season well. Place on large plates.

4 Cut the salmon into thick slices and serve on top of the leaves with the mustard butter spooned over.

Freezing: not suitable

Hot Rosemary Ciabatta

200 cals per serving

1 ready-to-bake ciabatta or French baguette

60 ml (4 tbsp) olive oil

few sprigs fresh rosemary or 15 ml (1 tbsp) dried

1 Remove the bread from its packet. Cut the bread in half lengthways, then into chunks. Place on foil.

2 Drizzle the oil and rosemary over the bread, then wrap tightly. Cook at 230°C (450°F) mark 8 for 12-15 minutes.

Freezing: not suitable

Saffron Potatoes

120 cals per serving

900 g (2 lb) old potatoes

5 ml (1 tsp) saffron strands or 2 small sachets of ground

salt and pepper

1 Scrub the potatoes but do not peel. Cut into thick slices.

2 Place the potatoes in a saucepan with just enough salted water to cover. Add the saffron and boil, uncovered, for 10 minutes or until almost tender. Increase

Roast Salmon in Mustard Butter

the heat and bubble down the liquid until almost evaporated and the potatoes are tender (about 20 minutes cooking time in total).

3 Drain and serve immediately.

Freezing: not suitable

Chilled Grapes and Vignotte

300 cals per serving
120 cals per serving grapes with wine

The simplest way to finish any meal is to offer chilled grapes with oatcakes and just one wonderful cheese – Vignotte would be a good choice. This is a creamy, pasteurised cheese from the Champagne region of France. It's available in some supermarkets and delicatessens; you'll need at least 450 g (1 lb) for 6 – it vanishes quickly! If you feel your guests will be disappointed if there's no pudding, strip the grapes off their stalks and pour a chilled dessert wine such as Moscatel de Valencia over. (700 g (1½ lb) fruit will take 300 ml (10 fl oz) of wine.) Accompany with crème fraîche.

Easy
Christmas Eve Menu 2

Here's another menu which can be prepared with the minimum of fuss, leaving you lots of time to get on with the preparations for the next day. To make the Bagna Cauda starter, you simply whizz the ingredients together in a food processor, then heat the dip through gently. You can buy ready-prepared vegetables for the crudités to make life even easier. The pasta main course is quickly created in a single pan, while the cold dessert is just a matter of slicing up seasonal fruit adding brandy, lemon juice and sugar and chilling until required.

MENU FOR 6

Bagna Cauda

Smoked Platter with Warm Pasta Salad

Clementines in Brandy

COUNTDOWN

To serve at 8pm

7pm Prepare the Clementines In Brandy. Cover and chill. Make the Bagna Cauda and keep at room temperature. Prepare the crudités; store in the refrigerator.

7.40pm Cook the pasta. Arrange the smoked meat on plates. Complete the pasta salad.

about 8pm Warm through the Bagna Cauda and serve.

Bagna Cauda

Serve this warm dip in a dish that will retain the heat. Buy ready-prepared crudités or pick a colour theme such as red and green for vegetables which need little preparation – radishes, cucumber, peppers and cherry tomatoes are a few suggestions. Offer a selection of crisps and savouries with the crudités.

370 cals per serving

selection of fresh vegetable crudités
150 ml (5 fl oz) thick double cream
60 ml (4 tbsp) olive oil
2 garlic cloves
50 g (2 oz) can anchovy fillets
125 g (4 oz) walnut pieces
salt and pepper
anchovy fillet and chopped walnuts, to garnish

1 Prepare the crudités. Blend together all the ingredients, except the crudités, in a food processor until quite smooth, reserving one anchovy fillet for garnish.
2 Pour into a saucepan and warm through very gently, stirring continuously. Season with salt and pepper to taste.
3 Serve warm with the vegetable crudités, garnished with the reserved anchovy fillet and walnuts.

Freezing: not suitable

Smoked Platter with Warm Pasta Salad

680 cals per serving

350 g (12 oz) dried spaghettini (thin spaghetti)
salt and pepper
175 g (6 oz) sun-dried tomatoes in oil (you'll need a 280 g/10 oz jar)
120 ml (8 tbsp) olive oil, preferably from sun-dried tomatoes above
90 ml (6 tbsp) chopped fresh chives or spring onions
175 g (6 oz) creamy, soft goats' cheese
75 g (3 oz) freshly grated Parmesan cheese
about 225 g (8 oz) smoked venison, Parma ham or smoked Black Forest ham
goats' cheese, to serve (optional)

1 Cook the spaghettini in boiling salted water for about 10-12 minutes or until just tender. Roughly chop the sun-dried tomatoes.
2 Drain the spaghettini. Toss in the tomatoes, oil and chives. Return to the saucepan and fork through the goats' cheese over a low heat. Add the grated Parmesan cheese and adjust the seasoning.
3 Put 2 or 3 slices of smoked meat on each plate. Add the hot spaghettini and serve immediately. Accompany with a little extra goats' cheese, if wished.

Freezing: not suitable

Clementines in Brandy

140 cals per serving

10 clementines or other seedless 'easy peelers'

12 pitted dates or no-soak prunes

juice of 1 lemon

30 ml (2 tbsp) caster sugar

60 ml (4 tbsp) brandy

1 Peel the clementines. Remove as much pith as possible, then thickly slice into a bowl. Roughly slice the dates or prunes and stir into the clementines.

2 Stir the lemon juice, sugar and brandy into the fruit. Cover and chill until required.

Freezing: not suitable

Clementines in Brandy

TRADITIONAL CHRISTMAS MENU

Celebrate Christmas in traditional style with a glorious turkey roast and all the trimmings. Organising such a feast is easier than you might think, as long as you plan ahead – just follow the countdown timetable provided and you are guaranteed a sumptuous festive success.

MENU FOR 8

Twice-baked Goats' Cheese Soufflés

Turkey with Roast Onions and Madeira Gravy
Mushroom and Olive Stuffing
Sausage and Chestnut Stuffing
Cranberry and Orange Sauce
Roast Potatoes
Carrots and Parsnips
Brussels Sprouts
Bread Sauce

Christmas Pudding
Sabayon Sauce

COUNTDOWN

Early November
Make the pudding.

One week before
Make the tomato filling for the soufflés and chill. Calculate the thawing time of the turkey. Prepare the cranberry sauce.

22 December
Soak the pears and prunes for the sausage stuffing.

23 December
Make the Bread Sauce to the end of step 3. Cover and chill. Make the stuffings, cover and chill. Peel the onions for the turkey; refrigerate.

Christmas Eve
Cook the soufflés to the end of step 5; refrigerate. Cut the carrots and parsnips, cover with cold water and chill. Trim the sprouts and refrigerate. Make the Sabayon Sauce, cool and chill. Prepare the stock for gravy; simmer the giblets in a covered pan with 1.1 litres (2 pints) water, seasoning and a few vegetables for 2 hours or until about 600 ml (1 pint) stock remains. Strain, cool and refrigerate.

Christmas Day
To serve at 1pm (or 7pm)
9am (3pm) Preheat the oven. Stuff the turkey and complete to the end of step 3. Spoon the sausage stuffing into a loaf tin.
9.30am (3.30pm) Put the turkey in the oven to cook.
10am (4pm) Put the pudding on to steam (if steaming).
11am (5pm) Continue soufflés as in steps 6 and 7. Put the cranberry sauce in a serving dish. Put the pudding on to boil (if boiling).
11.30am (5.30pm) Put the potatoes in the oven. Remove the foil from the turkey and add the onions.
12.20pm (6.20pm) Put the sausage stuffing into the oven.
12.30pm (6.30pm) Test the turkey and remove from the oven if cooked. Tent with foil to keep warm. Raise the oven to 200°C (400°F) mark 6 to brown the potatoes then keep warm, uncovered. Continue the soufflés as in step 8. Make the gravy. Cook the vegetables. Cover; keep warm. Reheat the Bread Sauce and complete.
12.45pm (6.45pm) Uncover the sausage stuffing for the last 15 minutes.
1pm (7pm) Serve. Turn out the Christmas Pudding. Whisk the Sabayon Sauce well before serving.

PREPARING AND COOKING YOUR TURKEY

Thawing

A frozen turkey must be thoroughly thawed before cooking. Leave the frozen turkey in its bag and thaw at cool room temperature, not in the refrigerator. Remove any giblets as soon as they are loose – all giblets, except the livers, can be used to make stock for the gravy. To check that the bird is thawed, make sure that there are no ice crystals in the body cavity and that the legs are quite flexible. Once it is thoroughly thawed, cover and store in the refrigerator. Cook within 24 hours.

Stuffing

Loosely stuff the neck end only; stuffing the cavity can inhibit heat penetration and pose a health risk. The stuffing should be cold before it is put in the bird. (Also when making the stuffing, make sure the cooked vegetables are cold before mixing with any raw minced meat.) Do not be tempted to overfill the turkey with stuffing – remember that the stuffing will swell as it absorbs fat and moisture from the bird during cooking. Any extra stuffing can be baked separately in a covered dish for about 1 hour. Allow about 225 g (8 oz) stuffing for each 2.3 kg (5 lb) dressed weight of turkey and stuff just before cooking.

Trussing

Trussing keeps the bird in a neat compact shape for even roasting. It also keeps in the stuffing and makes carving easier. You will need a long trussing needle threaded with fine cotton string.

First fold the neck skin under the body, then fold the wing tips back and under so that they hold it in position. Put the bird on its back and push the legs well into the sides. Push the trussing needle into the bird through the second joint of the wing, right through the body and out through the corresponding joint on the opposite side. Insert the needle in the first joint of the wing, pushing it through the flesh at the back of the body (catching the wing tips and the neck skin) and out through the opposite side. Cut the string and tie the two ends together.

To truss the legs, re-thread the needle and push it in through the gristle at one side of the parson's nose. Pass the string over both legs and then through the gristle at the other side of the parson's nose. Take it behind the parson's nose and tie the ends together.

Cooking

Weigh the bird after stuffing. Calculate the complete cooking time to be ready 30 minutes before carving – this allows time for the meat to firm up, making carving easier. Spread the turkey with butter and season with salt and pepper. Wrap the bird loosely in a tent of foil, then cook in a preheated oven at 190°C (375°F) mark 5. Remove the foil about 1 hour before the end of the cooking time to brown. Baste the turkey regularly during cooking.

Testing

To check that the turkey is cooked through, insert a skewer into a thigh. If the juices run clear, the turkey is cooked; if not, return to the oven for a little longer.

Carving

If you remove the wishbone before stuffing the turkey, it will be easier to carve. With large turkeys, the breast is usually carved first (right through the stuffing) and the legs are removed afterwards and carved separately.

LEFTOVER TURKEY

Any leftover turkey is delicious served cold as part of a salad spread, but is equally tasty turned into a hot dish. Curried turkey is always popular – try the Turkey and Mango Curry on page 135 – or for something different, offer Turkey Meatballs with Cranberry Dressing on page 134. For post-Christmas entertaining, use leftover turkey to make party food – tiny Turkey and Chestnut Tarts (see page 110) are excellent canapés.

Always keep leftover turkey in the refrigerator.

Turkey Timetable

Oven-ready weight (at room temp)	Approx. thawing time	Cooking time, foil-wrapped	Approx. number of servings
550 g-1.4 kg (1¼-3 lb)	4-10 hr	1-1½ hr	2-4
1.4-2.3 kg (3-5 lb)	10-15 hr	1½-2 hr	4-6
2.3-3.6 kg (5-8 lb)	15-18 hr	2-3 hr	6-10
3.6-5 kg (8-11 lb)	18-20 hr	3-3½ hr	10-15
5-6.8 kg (11-15 lb)	20-24 hr	3½-4½ hr	15-20
6.8-9 kg (15-20 lb)	24-30 hr	4½-5 hr	20-30

Twice-baked Goats' Cheese Soufflés

425 cals per serving

TOMATO FILLING

2 garlic cloves

45 ml (3 tbsp) olive oil

30 ml (2 tbsp) tomato purée

400 g (14 oz) can chopped plum tomatoes

large sprig fresh thyme or 1.25 ml (¼ tsp) dried

salt and pepper

SOUFFLE

butter for greasing

50 g (2 oz) butter

50 g (2 oz) plain flour

300 ml (10 fl oz) milk

4 eggs, separated

225 g (8 oz) soft, creamy goats' cheese

300 ml (10 fl oz) double cream

oakleaf lettuce or fresh herbs, to garnish

Twice-baked Goats' Cheese Soufflés

1 To make the tomato filling, peel and crush the garlic. Heat the oil in a small saucepan and add the tomato purée and crushed garlic. Cook, stirring, for 1 minute. Add the tomatoes, thyme and salt and pepper. Bring to the boil, then simmer gently for 45 minutes or until the sauce is very thick. Set aside to cool.

2 Base-line and lightly butter eight 150 ml (5 fl oz) ramekin dishes.

3 To make the soufflé mixture, melt the butter in a saucepan and stir in the flour. Mix to a smooth paste. Blend in the milk and stir continually until the mixture boils and is smooth. Cool a little, then beat in the egg yolks and cheese. Season well with salt and pepper. Whisk the egg whites until holding soft peaks and fold into the cheese mixture.

4 Fill each ramekin two-thirds full with the soufflé mixture and place 10 ml (2 tsp) tomato filling in the centre of each. Cover with remaining soufflé mixture. Reserve the remaining tomato filling.

5 Place the ramekins in a roasting tin and add enough hot water to come halfway up the side of the dishes. Cook at 180°C (350°F) mark 4 for 20 minutes or until firm to the touch. Remove the ramekins from the roasting tin and allow to cool.

6 Run a round-bladed knife around the edge of the soufflés and carefully turn out into individual ovenproof dishes.

7 Add 10 ml (2 tsp) coarse ground pepper to the cream. Spoon 30-40 ml (2-3 tbsp) on top of each soufflé. Bake at 200°C (400°F) mark 6 for 20-25 minutes or until golden. Meanwhile, reheat the remaining tomato filling.

8 To serve, spoon a little tomato filling on top of each soufflé with a small piece of oakleaf lettuce or sprig of herb to garnish. Serve immediately.

Freezing: suitable at the end of step 5. Thaw overnight in the refrigerator and complete as directed.

Turkey with Roast Onions and Madeira Gravy

860 cals per serving

1 quantity Mushroom and Olive Stuffing (see right)

3.6 kg (8 lb) oven-ready turkey

900 g (2 lb) small onions or shallots

150 g (5 oz) butter

salt and pepper

15 ml (1 tbsp) oil

fresh herbs to garnish

MADEIRA GRAVY

30 ml (2 tbsp) plain flour

600 ml (1 pint) turkey stock

60 ml (4 tbsp) Madeira

1 Spoon some stuffing into the neck end of the turkey only. Shape into a neat, rounded end then tuck the neck skin under and sew or secure with a wooden skewer or cocktail stick. Weigh the turkey and calculate the cooking time (see chart on page 69).

2 Spoon any remaining stuffing into foil and seal. Refrigerate until required. Peel the onions.

3 Place the turkey in a roasting tin and spread with 125 g (4 oz) softened butter. Season with a little salt and plenty of pepper. Cover loosely with a large sheet of foil to make a 'tent'. In a non-stick frying pan, brown the onions well in the oil and remaining butter.

4 Cook the turkey at 190°C (375°F) mark 5 for the calculated cooking time, basting occasionally. About 1 hour before the end of the cooking time, remove the foil and add the onions to the tin with the turkey.

5 When the turkey is cooked remove it and the onions from the roasting tin, tipping slightly to let any juices run out. Cover with foil and leave to rest for 30 minutes.

6 Meanwhile, make the Madeira Gravy. Tilt the roasting tin and spoon off all but 30 ml (2 tbsp) fat, leaving the turkey juices. Place the tin over a low heat and whisk in the plain flour. Cook for 1-2 minutes, then slowly whisk in the turkey stock. Bring to the boil and simmer for 3-4 minutes until

smooth. Add the Madeira and season with salt and pepper. Strain to serve.

7 Arrange the onions around the turkey, garnish the bird with fresh herbs and serve.

Freezing: not suitable

Mushroom and Olive Stuffing

410 cals per serving

450 g (1 lb) streaky bacon

3 small onions or shallots

60 ml (4 tbsp) oil

350 g (12 oz) small brown-cap mushrooms

125 g (4 oz) arborio (risotto) rice

pinch powdered saffron

600 ml (1 pint) chicken stock

125 g (4 oz) pitted green olives

30 ml (2 tbsp) chopped flat-leaf parsley

2 eggs

salt and pepper

1 Coarsely chop the bacon; peel and chop the onions or shallots.

2 Heat 15 ml (1 tbsp) oil in a deep frying pan or shallow flameproof casserole dish and cook the bacon until crisp. Remove with a slotted spoon. Add 15 ml (1 tbsp) oil to the pan and cook the mushrooms over a high heat for 4-5 minutes. Drain, reserving the pan juices.

3 Heat a further 30 ml (2 tbsp) oil and add the onions. Cook, stirring, for 6-7 minutes, add the rice and saffron and stir over the heat for a further minute. Gradually add the boiling stock, allowing the rice to absorb the stock and swell after each addition.

4 Mix together all the ingredients and season well with salt and pepper; cool.

5 Use to stuff the neck end of the turkey, as described on left. Cook any remaining stuffing mixture separately in foil for about 1 hour.

Freezing: suitable

Sausage and Chestnut Stuffing

Serve this stuffing separately as an extra trimming to the roast turkey.

360 cals per serving

125 g (4 oz) dried pears

12 pitted dried prunes

450 g (1 lb) coarse pork sausages

1 small onion or 2 shallots

25 g (1 oz) butter

grated rind and juice of 1 lemon

30 ml (2 tbsp) chopped flat-leaf parsley

225 g (8 oz) cooked chestnuts, preferably vacuum-packed

50 g (2 oz) fresh brown breadcrumbs

1.25 ml (¼ tsp) each ground nutmeg, ground cloves, ground cinnamon and ground coriander

salt and pepper

1 Cut the pears into large pieces. Cover the pears and prunes with cold water and leave overnight.

2 Place the sausages in a saucepan and cover with cold water. Bring to the boil and cook gently for 15 minutes or until cooked through. Allow to cool a little in the liquid, then drain, skin and cut into large cubes.

3 Peel and chop the onion or shallots and fry in the butter for 7-8 minutes or until soft. Mix together all the ingredients, seasoning well with the spices, salt and pepper. Spoon into a loaf tin and cover with foil.

4 Cook at 190°C (375°F) mark 5 for 40 minutes. Uncover for the last 15 minutes of cooking time.

Freezing: suitable, using fresh not previously frozen sausagemeat. Thaw at cool room temperature.

Cranberry and Orange Sauce

110 cals per serving

1 orange

350 g (12 oz) fresh or frozen cranberries

175 g (6 oz) caster sugar

150 ml (5 fl oz) red wine

150 ml (5 fl oz) orange juice

1 Finely grate the orange rind and squeeze the juice. Set the rind aside. Place the cranberries, sugar, wine and both orange juices in a saucepan and bring to the boil. Simmer, uncovered, stirring occasionally, for 30 minutes.

2 Remove and reserve half the cranberries. Blend the remainder of the sauce until smooth. Return to the pan with the reserved cranberries and orange rind. Cool, cover and chill. Serve cold.

Freezing: suitable. Thaw overnight at cool room temperature.

Roast Potatoes

250 cals per serving

1.8 kg (4 lb) old potatoes

coarse sea salt

150 ml (5 fl oz) oil

1 Roughly chop the potatoes (peel if wished). Parboil in boiling, salted water for about 10 minutes.

2 Drain; roughen the potato edges using a fork or toss them in the pan or a colander.

3 Heat the oil in a roasting tin over the hob. Spoon in the potatoes, baste with the oil and sprinkle with coarse sea salt. Roast high in the oven at 190°C (375°F) mark 5 for about 1 hour, basting occasionally.

4 Serve sprinkled with coarse sea salt.

Freezing: not suitable

Turkey with Roast Onions and Madeira Gravy and all the trimmings

Carrots and Parsnips

130 cals per serving

700 g (1½ lb) parsnips
700 g (1½ lb) carrots
salt and pepper

1 Peel the parsnips and carrots, then cut the vegetables into long, thin batons.
2 Cook in boiling, salted water for about 10 minutes until tender, but still retaining their bite.
3 Drain, season with salt and pepper and serve.

Freezing: not suitable

Brussels Sprouts

120 cals per serving

1.4 kg (3 lb) Brussels sprouts
salt and pepper
50 g (2 oz) butter
60 ml (4 tbsp) chopped fresh chives

1 Cook the sprouts in boiling, salted water for 7-10 minutes until tender but retaining their bite.
2 Drain well and toss in the butter and chives. Season with salt and pepper and serve.

Freezing: not suitable

Bread Sauce

355 cals per serving

2 medium onions

6 whole cloves

600 ml (1 pint) milk

4 bay leaves

6 black peppercorns

salt and pepper

175 g (6 oz) fresh white breadcrumbs

300 ml (10 fl oz) single cream

125 g (4 oz) butter

10 ml (2 tsp) freshly grated nutmeg

60 ml (4 tbsp) crème fraîche

1 Peel the onions, leaving them whole, then stud with the cloves. Place the onions in a saucepan with the milk, bay leaves and peppercorns. Season with salt and pepper.

2 Bring to the boil, then remove from the heat. Pour into a bowl, cover and set aside for 3 hours.

3 Strain the milk into a saucepan. Over a low heat, gradually add the breadcrumbs. Bring to the boil, stirring. Simmer for 5 minutes or until the sauce thickens.

4 Gently reheat the sauce with the cream, butter, nutmeg and plenty of seasoning. Stir in the crème fraîche just before serving.

Freezing: suitable at the end of step 3. Thaw overnight at cool room temperature.

Christmas Pudding

445 cals per serving

50 g (2 oz) each blanched almonds, walnuts and brazil nuts

75 g (3 oz) carrots

75 g (3 oz) no-soak pitted dried prunes

125 g (4 oz) butter, softened

finely grated rind of 1 lemon

125 g (4 oz) soft dark brown sugar

2 eggs, beaten

350 g (12 oz) seedless raisins, currants and sultanas, mixed

25 g (1 oz) chopped mixed peel

50 g (2 oz) fresh brown breadcrumbs

125 g (4 oz) plain wholemeal flour

50 g (2 oz) plain white flour

15 ml (1 tbsp) ground mixed spice

200 ml (7 fl oz) Guinness

30 ml (2 tbsp) brandy

30 ml (2 tbsp) black treacle

butter for greasing

brandy, to serve

Sabayon Sauce, to accompany (see page 75)

1 Roughly chop the nuts; coarsely grate the carrots; snip the prunes into small pieces. Mix together the butter and lemon rind. Gradually beat in the sugar, then the eggs. Mix in the remaining ingredients, stirring well. Cover; leave in a cool place (not the refrigerator) overnight.

2 The next day, lightly grease a 1.4-1.6 litre (2½-2¾ pint) heatproof pudding basin and base-line with non-stick baking parchment. Beat the pudding mixture again and spoon into the basin. Pleat pieces of greaseproof paper and foil together and tie securely over the basin.

3 Steam the pudding basin for about 6 hours or stand it in a large saucepan filled with enough boiling water to come halfway up the sides of the basin. Cover and boil for about 4 hours. Cool the pudding completely, re-cover the basin with fresh greaseproof paper and foil, and refrigerate for up to 2 months.

4 On the day, steam the pudding for about 3 hours or boil for about 2 hours. Turn out onto a warm serving plate. Warm 60 ml (4 tbsp) brandy in a small saucepan, pour over the pudding and set alight. Baste with the flaming brandy, then serve, cut into wedges, accompanied by Sabayon Sauce.

Freezing: suitable, after 1 month's maturing. Thaw overnight at cool room temperature; reheat as directed in step 4.

Christmas Pudding with Sabayon Sauce

Sabayon Sauce

Precise sizes of the saucepan, bowl and boiling time have been given to ensure the syrup reaches the correct temperature before adding to the egg yolks.

115 cals per serving

75 g (3 oz) caster sugar

3 egg yolks

100 ml (4 fl oz) double cream

grated rind and juice of 1 lemon

1 Place the sugar and 100 ml (4 fl oz) water in a small saucepan, 15 cm (6 inches) in diameter. Dissolve the sugar slowly over a low heat. Increase the heat to high and boil for 7-8 minutes. The liquid should look very syrupy with large pea-size bubbles.

2 Place the egg yolks in a small bowl, 12.5-15 cm (5-6 inches) in diameter. With an electric whisk, beat the yolks together, pour on the hot syrup in a thin stream and whisk until thick, mousse-like and cool.

3 Whip the cream to stiff peaks, add the lemon rind and juice and whip again to soft peaks.

4 Fold the cream into the mousse. Cover; chill in the refrigerator overnight.

5 Whisk well before serving.

Freezing: suitable at the end of step 4. Thaw overnight in the refrigerator.

ALTERNATIVE ORIENTAL CHRISTMAS MENU

For a Christmas Day meal with a difference, try giving the turkey an Oriental twist with a menu that uses all the luscious tastes and colours of the East. Flavour the joint with ginger and serve with a tangy fruit sauce and stir-fried vegetables to create a menu that is bursting with exotic tastes.

MENU FOR 6

Oriental Turkey
Ginger Butter
Ginger Glaze
Apple and Plum Sauce
Quick Stir-fry

Brandy and Sultana Iced Cream

COUNTDOWN

Two or three weeks before
Make the Brandy and Sultana Iced Cream.

Christmas Eve
Make the Ginger Butter; complete step 1 of Oriental Turkey. Cover and refrigerate. Make the Ginger Glaze and Apple and Plum Sauce; refrigerate. Complete step 1 of the Quick Stir-fry; refrigerate in polythene bags.

Christmas Day
To serve at 1pm (or 7pm)
11.30am (5.30pm) Place the Brandy and Sultana Iced Cream in the refrigerator.

11.45am (5.45pm) Put the turkey in the oven.

12.30pm (6.30pm) Finish the Quick Stir-fry. Cover and keep warm if necessary.

12.45pm (6.45pm) Remove the turkey from the oven and allow to stand for 15 minutes. Gently heat through the Apple and Plum Sauce.

1pm (7pm) Serve the meal.

Oriental Turkey

765 cals per serving, including butter and glaze

1 quantity Ginger Butter (see page 78)

1.8 kg (4 lb) oven-ready turkey saddle or breast

1 quantity Ginger Glaze (see page 78)

lychees and limes, to decorate

Apple and Plum Sauce, to serve (see page 78)

1 Weigh the turkey saddle or breast and calculate the cooking time according to 15 minutes per 450 g (1 lb). Soften the Ginger Butter, then carefully loosen the turkey skin and push the butter evenly underneath.

2 Place the turkey in a roasting tin and brush with Ginger Glaze. Cover with foil and cook at 190°C (375°F) mark 5 for the calculated time. Baste the turkey frequently with Ginger Glaze.

3 Uncover the turkey for the last 15 minutes to brown the skin. Baste again with any remaining Ginger Glaze over the breast at this stage.

4 Rest the turkey for 15 minutes before carving. Serve with Apple and Plum Sauce.

Freezing: not suitable

Ginger Butter

155 cals per serving

5 cm (2 inch) piece fresh root ginger
125 g (4 oz) butter, softened
salt and pepper

1 Peel and finely grate the ginger. Beat together with the butter. Season well with salt and pepper.

Freezing: suitable. Thaw overnight at cool room temperature.

Ginger Glaze

This glaze is also delicious with roast ham, pork or beef.

50 cals per serving

5 cm (2 inch) piece fresh root ginger
30 ml (2 tbsp) light soy sauce
30 ml (2 tbsp) rice or distilled malt vinegar
90 ml (6 tbsp) clear honey
salt and pepper

1 Peel and finely grate the ginger. Mix together all the ingredients and season with salt and pepper to taste.

Freezing: not suitable

Apple and Plum Sauce

This recipe makes 1.3 litres (2¼ pints) of sauce.

30 cals per 15 ml (1 tbsp)

1.8 kg (4 lb) Golden Delicious apples
60 ml (4 tbsp) caster sugar
grated rind and juice of 2 limes
150 ml (5 fl oz) ready-made plum sauce
salt and pepper
chopped red chillies, to garnish

1 Peel, core and chop the apples.
2 Cook the apples over a low heat with the sugar and 150 ml (5 fl oz) water until soft. Add the lime rind, juice and plum sauce; stir well.
3 Purée in a blender until smooth. Season with salt and pepper. Reheat gently to serve hot, or serve cold. Garnish with chopped chillies.

Freezing: suitable, without garnish. Thaw overnight at cool room temperature.

Quick Stir-fry

225 cals per serving

2-3 large red peppers, about 550 g (1¼ lb) total weight
3 large bunches spring onions
550 g (1¼ lb) red cabbage
two 227 g cans water chestnuts
25 ml (1 fl oz) oil
350 g (12 oz) beansprouts
200 ml (7 fl oz) rice or distilled malt vinegar
15-30 ml (1-2 tbsp) ready-made chilli sauce
125 g (4 oz) caster sugar
salt and pepper

Brandy and Sultana Iced Cream

1 Deseed the peppers and slice into matchsticks. Slice the spring onions diagonally. Finely shred the cabbage. Drain the water chestnuts and slice horizontally.

2 Heat the oil in a wok; when smoking, stir-fry the spring onions, beansprouts and water chestnuts for 2-3 minutes over a high heat. Remove from the wok and set aside.

3 Stir-fry the peppers and cabbage. Stir in the vinegar, chilli sauce and sugar. Season with salt and pepper. Stir-fry over a high heat for 5-10 minutes.

4 Return the spring onion mixture to the wok; toss over a high heat for 1 minute. Adjust seasoning and serve.

Freezing: not suitable

Brandy and Sultana Iced Cream

580 cals per serving

125 g (4 oz) sultanas or raisins

100 ml (4 fl oz) brandy

100 ml (4 fl oz) crème de cacao

600 ml (1 pint) double cream

pinch freshly grated nutmeg

icing sugar, to sweeten

1 Soak the sultanas in the alcohol for 1 hour. Lightly whip the cream until it just holds its shape. Fold in the sultanas, alcohol, nutmeg and icing sugar to taste.

2 Cover and freeze. To serve, place in the refrigerator 2 hours before serving.

Freezing: suitable

ALTERNATIVE ROAST CHRISTMAS MENU

In this spectacular menu, a luxurious roast fillet of beef is offered as an alternative to the traditional turkey. The mood of the menu is still very festive and the food is easy to serve, making it ideal for a celebratory gathering.

MENU FOR 8

Smoked Fish Terrine

Festive Fillet of Beef
Red Cabbage with Pine Nuts
Potato and Celeriac Galette

Brûléed Citrus Tart

COUNTDOWN

Two days before
Prepare the terrine to the end of step 6 and chill. Prepare the pastry case and bake blind; cool, store in an airtight container. Make the citrus curd for the tart as in step 3. Cover and chill.

Christmas Eve
Soak the raisins for the beef. Prepare the shallots and refrigerate in a polythene bag. Shred the red cabbage, peel and grate the ginger root; refrigerate together in a polythene bag.

Christmas Day
To serve at 1pm (7pm)
9am Prepare the beef to the end of step 4, cover and refrigerate. Complete the filling and grill the Brûléed Citrus Tart. Prepare the bread and butter accompaniment for the terrine. Cover in cling film and refrigerate. Make the cucumber relish for the terrine.
About 11.15am (5.15pm) Peel and slice the potatoes and celeriac; complete the recipe and bake.
About 12.15pm (6.15pm) Complete beef recipe and roast, cooking for 5-10 minutes less than suggested in the recipe, as the beef will continue to cook while it is being kept warm in the low oven. Complete the red cabbage recipe. Turn out the Smoked Fish Terrine and refrigerate.
12.45pm (6.45pm) Turn out the galettes. Turn oven down to low and keep food warm.
1pm (7pm) Serve the meal. Decorate the Brûléed Citrus Tart just before serving.

Smoked Fish Terrine

Try serving this terrine with tiny sandwiches made from brown bread, spread with unsalted butter flavoured with a little lemon juice, and a filling of chopped fresh herbs.

285 cals per serving

450 g (1 lb) smoked haddock

½ onion

1 bay leaf

few peppercorns

100 ml (4 fl oz) double cream

30 ml (2 tbsp) chopped fresh dill

5 ml (1 tsp) paprika

2.5 ml (½ tsp) cayenne pepper

30 ml (2 tbsp) lemon juice

salt and pepper

11 g (0.4 oz) packet powdered gelatine

175-225 g (6-8 oz) smoked trout, thinly sliced

75-125 g (3-4 oz) boneless smoked trout fillets

75-125 g (3-4 oz) boneless smoked mackerel fillets

CUCUMBER RELISH

½ cucumber

75 ml (3 fl oz) light olive oil

45 ml (3 tbsp) lemon juice

15 ml (1 tbsp) chopped fresh dill

1 Put the smoked haddock in a shallow pan, and add sufficient cold water to just cover. Peel and slice the onion. Add to the pan with the bay leaf and peppercorns. Bring to the boil, lower the heat and poach gently for 15 minutes or until the fish flakes easily.

2 Remove the fish from the pan. Strain and reserve 100 ml (4 fl oz) of the poaching liquid. Flake the fish, removing any bones; leave to cool.

3 Place the flaked smoked haddock, cream, dill, paprika, cayenne and lemon juice in a food processor and blend until smooth. Season with salt and pepper.

4 Put the reserved liquid in a small pan and sprinkle on the gelatine. Leave to soak for 5 minutes, then dissolve over a very low heat. Stir into the fish mixture.

5 Lightly oil a 900 ml (1½ pint) terrine or loaf tin and line with cling film. Line the base and sides with the smoked trout slices, reserving some for the top. Remove the skin from the trout and mackerel fillets, then halve lengthways.

6 Spoon a third of the puréed fish mixture into the bottom of the terrine and spread evenly. Lay half the trout and mackerel fillets on top, then cover with half the remaining puréed mixture. Repeat with the remaining fish fillets and puréed mixture, smoothing the surface. Cover with the rest of the smoked trout slices. Chill in the refrigerator for at least 3 hours, until firm.

7 To make the relish, halve the cucumber lengthways and scoop out the seeds, using a teaspoon. Finely dice the cucumber flesh. Whisk together the oil and lemon juice in a bowl. Stir in the dill and diced cucumber, then season with salt and pepper.

8 To serve, turn out the terrine onto a board and remove the cling film. Cut into slices and serve with salad leaves.

Freezing: suitable at the end of step 6. Thaw overnight and complete as directed.

VARIATIONS

Use smoked salmon rather than smoked trout to line the tin. Smoked cod can be used in place of the haddock.

Festive Fillet of Beef

Ask your butcher to give you the middle cut of the fillet to avoid getting any thin tail ends.

The shallots are simply trimmed, not peeled. This gives good colour to the beef juices, while the shallots keep their shape and are soft and juicy inside.

Lexia raisins are much larger and fatter than the normal variety. They're available from most health food shops.

420 cals per serving

125 g (4 oz) Lexia raisins or sultanas

200 ml (7 fl oz) Madeira

75 g (3 oz) thinly sliced Parma ham

30 ml (2 tbsp) roughly chopped fresh parsley

1.1 kg (2½ lb) fillet of beef

350 g (12 oz) aubergine

A serving of Festive Fillet of Beef

about 100 ml (4 fl oz) olive oil

700 g (1½ lb) shallots or small onions

5 ml (1 tsp) each ground ginger and allspice

15 ml (1 tbsp) light muscovado sugar

150 ml (5 fl oz) beef stock

1 Soak the raisins or sultanas in the Madeira overnight. Drain well, reserving the Madeira.

2 Cut the Parma ham into 12 long strips about 2.5 cm (1 inch) wide. Dip 12 raisins in half the roughly chopped parsley, then roll each one tightly in a strip of ham.

3 Using the point of a sharp knife, make 12 small, deep incisions into the beef. Push in the Parma ham rolls. Tie the beef at 2.5 cm (1 inch) intervals with fine string to produce a neat shape.

4 Thinly slice the aubergine lengthways and brush lightly with a little of the oil. Grill for 2-3 minutes each side until golden brown. Cool. Trim the root ends of the shallots, but

don't remove completely. Halve any large ones or quarter the onions.

5 Heat 45 ml (3 tbsp) olive oil in a flameproof casserole or roasting tin. Brown the fillet all over, then remove and set aside.

6 Add another 15 ml (1 tbsp) oil to the pan with the spices and shallots. Sauté for 3-4 minutes or until golden brown, stirring the mixture occasionally.

7 Cover the fillet with the aubergine and return to the pan. Mix together the reserved Madeira, sugar, stock and remaining raisins and pour over the fillet. Bring to the boil and season.

8 Cook, uncovered, at 230°C (450°F) mark 8 for 35-40 minutes for medium rare. Allow a further 10-12 minutes for well done. Stir the remaining parsley into the pan juices. Slice the beef as thinly as possible and serve with warmed pan juices.

Freezing: not suitable

Red Cabbage with Pine Nuts

Balsamic vinegar is a wonderful sweet-and-sour vinegar, now widely available in many supermarkets.

135 cals per serving

900 g (2 lb) red cabbage

2.5 cm (1 inch) piece fresh root ginger (optional)

25 ml (1 fl oz) olive oil

150 ml (5 fl oz) light stock

salt and pepper

40 g (1½ oz) butter

30 ml (2 tbsp) Balsamic vinegar or red wine vinegar plus 10 ml (2 tsp) muscovado sugar

50 g (2 oz) toasted pine nuts

1 Shred the red cabbage very finely. Peel and grate the root ginger, if using.

2 Heat the oil in a large saucepan and sauté the cabbage with the ginger over a high heat for 3-4 minutes or until reduced in bulk, stirring occasionally.

3 Add the stock and season with salt and pepper. Bring to the boil, then cover and cook over a low heat for about 20 minutes. Stir occasionally.

4 When the cabbage is just tender, uncover and bubble down any excess liquid. Off the heat, stir in the butter, balsamic vinegar and pine nuts. Adjust the seasoning, cover and keep warm.

Freezing: not suitable

Potato and Celeriac Galette

200 cals per serving

75 g (3 oz) melted butter, plus extra for greasing

900 g (2 lb) old potatoes

900 g (2 lb) celeriac

1 large garlic clove

freshly grated nutmeg

salt and pepper

chopped fresh parsley, to garnish

1 Grease and base-line two 20.5 cm (8 inch) sandwich tins with non-stick baking parchment.

2 Peel and very thinly slice the potatoes and celeriac, preferably in a food processor. Peel and crush the garlic.

3 Layer up the vegetables with the crushed garlic, nutmeg and salt and pepper, pressing down firmly as you go – the tins will be very full. Pour about 40 g (1½ oz) melted butter over each one.

4 Cover with foil and bake at 230°C (450°F) mark 8 for 1¼ hours until the vegetables are quite tender. Test with a skewer.

5 Turn the galettes out onto a serving plate. Keep warm, uncovered. Garnish with parsley.

Freezing: not suitable

Brûléed Citrus Tart

This tart is very rich, so serve in small fingers. Any left over will keep well in the refrigerator for up to two days.

665 cals per serving

125 g (4 oz) unsalted butter

225 g (8 oz) plain white flour

125 g (4 oz) caster sugar

4 egg yolks, beaten

FILLING

4 whole eggs

4 egg yolks

125 g (4 oz) caster sugar

finely grated rind and juice of 2 lemons

finely grated rind and juice of 1 large orange

2 passion fruit

50 g (2 oz) unsalted butter

300 ml (10 fl oz) double cream

icing sugar

quartered figs and lemon and lime slices, to decorate

Brûléed Citrus Tart

1 First make the pastry. Rub the fat into the flour until the mixture resembles fine breadcrumbs. Stir in the sugar and bind to a dough with the egg yolks. Knead lightly; wrap and chill for about 30 minutes.

2 Roll out the pastry and use to line a 23 cm (9 inch), 3 cm (1¼ inch) deep loose-based fluted flan tin. Chill, then bake blind until golden brown and well dried out.

3 Meanwhile, make the citrus curd. In a bowl, beat or whisk together the whole eggs and egg yolks with the caster sugar. Add the finely grated rinds of the lemons and orange with 90 ml (6 tbsp) each lemon and orange juice. Halve the passion fruit, scoop the seeds and pulp into a sieve and squeeze the juice into the bowl. Place the bowl over a pan of simmering water and cook gently, stirring or whisking frequently until the curd thickens slightly and

coats the back of the spoon. Do not boil. Take off the heat and whisk in the butter until melted. Cool. Whisk the cream until it just holds its shape, then fold into the curd mixture. Cover and chill.

4 Spoon the curd into the flan case. Dredge the curd filling with icing sugar. Protect the pastry edge with a strip of foil, then flash the flan under a very hot grill until the sugar begins to caramelise. Leave to cool.

5 Chill the tart for several hours before decorating with quartered figs and lemon and lime slices.

Freezing: suitable; pack and freeze the pastry case at the end of step 2. Thaw for 2 hours. Pack and freeze the curd filling separately. Thaw at cool room temperature for about 6 hours. Complete as directed above.

VEGETARIAN CHRISTMAS MENU

This menu proves that a meal without meat can be just as festive and memorable as the traditional fare offered at Christmas time.

A fresh-tasting starter of crisp Parmesan wafers, layered with lettuce and a tangy dressing, contrasts brilliantly with the sumptuous main course – layers of spinach, artichoke hearts and chestnuts encased in light pastry and served with a rich thyme and port gravy. A glorious creamy gâteau, flavoured with coffee and chocolate, rounds off the meal in style.

The gâteau will in fact feed 10 people which allows for second helpings. Alternatively, any left over can be served the next day or can be frozen for another meal.

MENU FOR 6

Parmesan Wafers with Chilli Salad

Chestnut and Artichoke en Croûte with Thyme and Port Gravy

Sweet Potato Mash

Tiramisu Gâteau

COUNTDOWN

Three Days Before
Make the Thyme and Port Gravy, cool quickly and store in the refrigerator.

Two Days Before
Make the Parmesan Wafers and store in an airtight container. Make the chilli dressing and keep in a cool place. Coarsely shred the cos lettuce and store in a polythene bag in the refrigerator. Make the sponge layers for the Tiramisu Gâteau and store in an airtight tin. Make the chocolate waves for the gâteau and chill.

Christmas Eve
Assemble the gâteau as in steps 4-6 and chill. Prepare the Chestnut and Artichoke en Croûte up to the end of step 4 – refrigerate the stuffing and store the cooked pastry in an airtight tin. Remove the chilled gâteau from the tin and return to the refrigerator to chill overnight.

Christmas Day
To serve at 1pm (or 7pm).
9am (3pm) Roll out the remaining pastry for the en croûte and assemble the dish as in steps 5 and 6. Cover with cling film and chill.
12pm (6pm) Dust the gâteau with cocoa and decorate with chocolate waves. Cook the sweet potatoes, then mash, cover and keep warm.
12.15pm (6.15pm) Preheat the oven.
12.30pm (6.30pm) Put the Chestnut and Artichoke en Croûte in the oven. Bring the gravy to the boil, simmer for 1-2 minutes; keep warm.
12.50pm (6.50pm) Check the en croûte and remove from the oven if cooked. Tent with foil to keep warm. Reheat the Parmesan Wafers until crisp. Toss the lettuce with dressing and assemble the starter.
1pm (7pm) Serve the starter.

Parmesan Wafers with Chilli Salad

Parmesan Wafers with Chilli Salad

350 cals per serving

275 g (10 oz) freshly grated Parmesan cheese

about 50 g (2 oz) semolina

1 red chilli

1 garlic clove

75 ml (3 fl oz) extra-virgin olive oil

30 ml (2 tbsp) white wine vinegar

salt and pepper

1 cos lettuce

Parmesan shavings, to serve

1 Place a small non-stick crêpe pan over a moderate to high heat. Sprinkle a thin, lacy covering of grated Parmesan over the pan base. Add a sprinkling of semolina. Leave for about 30 seconds until the cheese begins to bubble. Sprinkle over a second thin layer of cheese and semolina and leave for 1 minute until the cheese melts and turns pale golden.

2 Remove from the heat and leave to cool for about 30 seconds. As the cheese firms, push the tip of a round-bladed knife underneath it to loosen. Ease out of the pan and leave to cool on a wire rack.

3 Use the remaining cheese and semolina to make 12 wafers. Store in an airtight container.

4 Deseed and finely chop the chilli. Peel and crush the garlic. Whisk the chilli and garlic with the olive oil and vinegar. Season well with salt and pepper.

5 Coarsely shred the lettuce. To assemble each serving, top a Parmesan wafer with some lettuce, drizzle over the dressing and sprinkle with Parmesan shavings. Top with a second wafer. Serve immediately.

Chestnut and Artichoke en Croûte

Chestnut and Artichoke en Croûte

560 cals per serving

75 g (3 oz) shallots

225 g (8 oz) mixed mushrooms

100 g (3½ oz) cooked chestnuts

3 garlic cloves

100 g (3½ oz) spinach leaves

50 g (2 oz) butter

45 ml (3 tbsp) balsamic vinegar

5 ml (1 tsp) chopped fresh thyme

150 ml (5 fl oz) double cream

salt and pepper

200 g (7 oz) can artichoke hearts

500 g (1 lb 1 oz) puff pastry

1 egg, beaten

Thyme and Port Gravy (see page 89), to serve

1 Peel and roughly chop the shallots; roughly chop the mushrooms and chestnuts; peel and crush the garlic. Plunge the spinach into boiling water for 1-2 seconds, then drain and refresh with cold water. Dry the spinach on kitchen paper.

2 Melt the butter in a saucepan. Add the shallots and cook, stirring, for 2-3 minutes. Add the mushrooms and cook for 3-4 minutes. Stir in the garlic and vinegar and cook for 1 minute. Add the chestnuts, thyme and double cream. Bring to the boil and bubble for 10 minutes to a sticky glaze. Season well with salt and pepper, then cool the mixture slightly.

3 Drain and roughly chop the artichokes, then stir into the chestnut mixture. Place cling film on the work surface and cover with half the spinach to form a rectangle 20.5 x 15 cm (8 x 6 inches). Season with salt and pepper, then spread with half the chestnut mixture. Roll and wrap tightly using cling film to 'seal'. Repeat with the remaining spinach and chestnut stuffing. Chill.

4 Roll out 125 g (4 oz) puff pastry to a rectangle 30.5 x 20.5 cm (12 x 8 inches). Place on a baking sheet and prick well; chill for 30 minutes. Cook at 220°C (425°F) mark 7 for 15 minutes or until golden. Cool, then cut the pastry in half to give two rectangles 20.5 x 15 cm (8 x 6 inches).

5 Remove the cling film from the spinach and stuffing rolls, and place one on each piece of pastry, trimming the pastry to the same size.

6 Thinly roll out 375 g (13 oz) puff pastry to a rectangle about 56 x 23 cm (22 x 9 inches). Halve to give two rectangles 28 x 23 cm (11 x 9 inches). Brush the pastry with beaten egg, then wrap the pastry, egg-side down, around the spinach. Trim, allowing 2.5 cm (1 inch) excess to tuck under the pastry bases. Brush with beaten egg and use the trimmings for decoration. Cover with cling film; chill for at least 30 minutes. Brush with beaten egg.

7 Cook at 230°C (450°F) mark 8 for 20-30 minutes. If the pastry starts to turn too brown, cover with foil. Stand for 5 minutes, then serve with the gravy.

Freezing: suitable at the end of step 6. Thaw overnight at cool room temperature and complete step 7.

Thyme and Port Gravy

Strict vegetarians should use crusted port or vegetarian red wine for this recipe.

85 cals per serving

50 g (2 oz) each leek, celery, onion and carrot

30 ml (2 tbsp) oil

300 ml (10 fl oz) red wine

1.7 litres (3 pints) vegetable stock

5 ml (1 tsp) chopped fresh thyme

150 ml (5 fl oz) port

5 ml (1 tsp) redcurrant jelly

salt and pepper

1 Clean and chop the leek and celery; peel and chop the onion and carrot. Heat the oil in a large saucepan. Add the vegetables and cook over a high heat, stirring, for 10 minutes or until the vegetables are coloured.

2 Add the wine and boil to reduce by half. Add the stock and thyme, bring to the boil and simmer, uncovered, for 1 hour. Strain and return to the rinsed-out pan.

3 Add the port and jelly. Boil the stock briskly for 20-30 minutes or until syrupy – there should be about 450 ml (15 fl oz). Season with salt and pepper.

Freezing: suitable. Thaw overnight at cool room temperature. Bring to the boil and simmer for 1-2 minutes.

Sweet Potato Mash

340 cals per serving

1.1 kg (2½ lb) sweet potatoes

salt and pepper

50 ml (2 fl oz) extra-virgin olive oil

150 ml (5 fl oz) double cream

1 Peel and roughly chop the sweet potatoes. Cook in boiling, salted water for about 20 minutes or until tender. Drain, return the potatoes to the pan and shake over the heat.

2 Mash the potatoes over heat and beat in the olive oil and cream, a little at a time. Season with salt and pepper and serve.

Freezing: not suitable

Tiramisu Gâteau

To make the chocolate waves decoration, simply spread about 30 ml (2 tbsp) melted chocolate over the back of a baking sheet. Freeze for 1-2 minutes then allow 20 seconds to bring to room temperature. Push the sharp edge of a wallpaper stripping knife, at an angle, into and along the chocolate, moving the blade from left to right to form large waves. Chill to set.

470 cals per serving

melted vegetable fat for greasing

125 g (4 oz) strong plain white flour, plus extra for dusting

200 g (7 oz) caster sugar, plus extra for dusting

6 eggs, size 2

two 250 g (9 oz) tubs mascarpone cheese

5 ml (1 tsp) vanilla essence

150 ml (5 fl oz) double cream

100 g (4 oz) milk chocolate

100 ml (4 fl oz) cold strong black coffee

100 ml (4 fl oz) Tia Maria or any other coffee-flavoured liqueur

cocoa powder, to dust

chocolate waves, to decorate

1 Grease 3 baking sheets and dust with a little flour and sugar. Place 4 eggs and 175 g (6 oz) sugar in a large bowl. Whisk with an electric whisk until the mixture is pale, thick and creamy. Sift in the flour and fold in gently.

2 Spread the mixture on the baking sheets into three circles of about 25.5 cm (10 inches).

3 Bake at 200°C (400°F) mark 6 for about 10 minutes or until lightly risen, pale golden brown and firm to the touch. Cool for about 30 seconds. Loosen carefully with a palette knife and slide onto wire racks lined with non-stick baking parchment to complete cooling.

4 Meanwhile, separate the remaining 2 eggs. Whisk the egg yolks with 25 g (1 oz) sugar, the cheese and vanilla essence until well blended. Lightly whisk the cream and fold in. Whisk the egg whites until they stand in peaks, then fold into the cheese mixture. Cover and refrigerate until required.

5 Coarsely grate the chocolate and set aside. Mix the coffee and liqueur together.

6 Trim the sponges into 23 cm (9 inch) rounds. Base-line a 23 cm (9 inch) spring-release cake tin with non-stick baking parchment. Place one sponge round, smooth-side down, in the base. Spoon over one-third of the coffee mixture. Sprinkle over half the chocolate, then spoon over half the cheese mixture. Continue layering the ingredients, ending with a sponge round, soaked in coffee mixture. Cover and refrigerate for about 5 hours.

7 Remove from the tin and refrigerate overnight.

8 To serve, dust the gâteau with cocoa and decorate with chocolate waves.

Freezing: suitable, after removing from the tin in step 7. Thaw at cool room temperature for 4 hours, then complete as in step 8.

Tiramisu Gâteau

PREPARE-AHEAD BOXING DAY MENU

A menu that can be prepared well in advance is perfect for a relaxing Boxing Day get-together.
Both the main course and dessert can be frozen well ahead of time,
leaving very little last-minute preparation on the day.
A delicious salmon pie served with fresh-tasting salads is also just what is called for after
a day of feasting on Christmas fare!

MENU FOR 8

**Salmon Pie with Parmesan
Crust
Bay-roasted Potatoes
Fennel and Cucumber Salad
Christmas Salad**

**Lime and Cranberry Ice
Tuiles**

COUNTDOWN

Well ahead
Prepare and freeze the salmon pie, Lime and Cranberry Ice, cranberries in syrup
and Tuiles.

A few days ahead
Make the salad dressings; cover and store in a cool place.

The day before
Make the Fennel and Cucumber Salad

Boxing Day
To serve at 1pm (7pm)
Early Scrub the potatoes. Rinse, drain and dry the salad leaves, refrigerate in
polythene bags. Slice the onions into rings, refrigerate in a polythene bag. Prepare
the pomegranate, cover and refrigerate.
11am (5pm) Preheat the oven to 190°C (375°F) mark 5.
11.15am (5.15pm) Put the salmon pie in the oven to bake.
11.45am (5.45pm) Complete the Bay-roasted Potatoes.
About 12pm (6pm) Put the ice cream in the refrigerator to begin softening. Place
the frozen Tuiles on a plate, ready to serve. Just before serving, toss the
Christmas Salad.

Salmon Pie with Parmesan Crust

This pie can be cooked from the freezer so it's ideal for last-minute entertaining. Don't expect a completely smooth sauce – it's a tasty mix topped with a crisp cheese crust.

720 cals per serving

900 g (2 lb) salmon fillet, skinned

125 g (4 oz) Gruyère cheese

50 g (2 oz) onion

225 g (8 oz) butter

400 g (14 oz) plain white flour

450 ml (15 fl oz) fish stock

150 ml (5 fl oz) dry white wine

225 g (8 oz) queen scallops (optional)

salt and pepper

75 g (3 oz) freshly grated Parmesan cheese

1 egg, beaten

beaten egg, to glaze

chopped fresh herbs, to garnish (optional)

1 Cut the salmon into large bite-sized pieces. Grate the Gruyère cheese. Peel and finely chop the onion.

2 Melt 50 g (2 oz) butter in a medium saucepan. Sauté the onion, stirring, for 5-6 minutes or until softened but not coloured.

3 Off the heat, stir in 50 g (2 oz) flour, the stock and wine. Bring to the boil, stirring, then simmer for 3-4 minutes until thickened. Remove from the heat and allow to cool slightly.

4 Add the salmon, scallops, if using, and Gruyère cheese. Season with salt and pepper, then turn into a 1.7 litre (3 pint) shallow, ovenproof dish and cool.

5 Rub 175 g (6 oz) butter into 350 g (12 oz) flour. Stir in the Parmesan. Add the beaten egg and 45-60 ml (3-4 tbsp) cold water. Bind the pastry together with your hands, adding extra water, if necessary.

6 Turn out onto a floured surface and knead lightly until smooth. Cover and chill for about 15 minutes.

7 Roll out the pastry and use to cover the filling, pressing the edges down well. Trim the excess pastry and re-roll.

8 Cut out holly leaves from the trimmings. Brush the pie with beaten egg and decorate with the pastry leaves.

Brush with egg again. Chill for 15-20 minutes.

9 Bake at 190°C (375°F) mark 5 for 45-50 minutes or until crisp, covering loosely with foil if necessary. Serve immediately, sprinkling herbs over each serving, if wished.

Freezing: suitable – ensure that the sauce (step 3) is quite cold before stirring in the fish. Do not use previously frozen fish. Complete the pie to the end of step 8, then open-freeze. Overwrap once firm. Cook from frozen at 190°C (375°F) mark 5 for about 1¾ hours. Cover lightly with foil towards the end of cooking.

Bay-roasted Potatoes

The bay leaves inserted into the potatoes add a really delicious flavour. If you're short of time, simply add a few bay leaves to the roasting tin with the oil and garlic.

240 cals per serving

1.4 kg (3 lb) small, even-sized potatoes

rock salt and pepper

about 10-12 fresh or dried bay leaves

2 garlic cloves

about 75 ml (3 fl oz) olive oil

1 Scrub the potatoes if necessary, but don't peel. Cook in boiling, salted water for 2 minutes. Drain and cool for 1-2 minutes. Slit 10-12 of the potatoes and insert a bay leaf.

2 Meanwhile, peel and crush the garlic and place, with the olive oil, in one large or two medium roasting tins. Heat in the oven at 190°C (375°F) mark 5 for 3-4 minutes. Toss in the hot potatoes, then shake them well in the tins until they are coated in olive oil. Season with the rock salt and pepper.

3 Roast the potatoes for about 35-40 minutes or until they are golden brown and tender. Serve hot with some extra rock salt sprinkled over, if wished.

Freezing: not suitable

Fennel and Cucumber Salad on the left; Christmas Salad on the right

Fennel and Cucumber Salad

If Florence fennel is unobtainable, use three medium cucumbers for this salad. It may sound a lot, but the thinly sliced cucumber softens down quite considerably in the dressing.

85 cals per serving

30 ml (2 tbsp) caster sugar

50 ml (2 fl oz) lemon juice

50 ml (2 fl oz) olive oil

salt and pepper

3 large heads Florence fennel, about 700 g (1½ lb) total weight

45 ml (3 tbsp) chopped fresh parsley

1 cucumber

1 Whisk together the first four ingredients.

2 Trim the leafy ends from the fennel and finely chop them. Stir into the lemon and oil mixture with the fresh parsley.

3 Thinly slice the fennel and cucumber. Toss in the herb dressing until evenly coated. Cover and chill for at least 1 hour, preferably overnight.

Freezing: not suitable

Christmas Salad

65 cals per serving

Rocket, with its strong peppery flavour, gives this salad a refreshing tang, but watercress would be an excellent substitute, or try a mixture of salad leaves. The most important thing is to choose some very green leaves to provide a contrast with the red-skinned onions and pomegranate.

2 red-skinned onions

1 pomegranate

1 large bunch rocket or 3 bunches watercress, or a mixture of both

50 ml (2 fl oz) olive oil

30 ml (2 tbsp) red wine vinegar

10 ml (2 tsp) Dijon mustard

salt and pepper

1 Peel and thinly slice the onions into rings. Halve and open the pomegranate and separate out the seeds, discarding all the pith and membrane. Trim, rinse, drain and dry the salad leaves.

2 Whisk together the oil, vinegar, mustard and salt and pepper. Toss with the salad leaves, onion rings and pomegranate. Serve immediately.

Freezing: not suitable

Lime and Cranberry Ice

If using fresh cranberries, slightly soften them over a low heat. Add a little water to stop them sticking, then strain.

270 cals per serving

8 egg yolks

225 g (8 oz) caster sugar

450 ml (15 fl oz) milk

500 g (1 lb 2 oz) carton bio natural yogurt

550 g (1¼ lb) frozen cranberries, thawed

grated rind and juice of 2 limes

juice of 1 orange

1 Whisk together the egg yolks and 175 g (6 oz) sugar until thick and pale. Bring the milk to just below boiling; pour onto the egg mixture, whisking continuously. Rinse out the pan.

2 Return the mixture to the pan and heat gently, stirring, until the custard thickens slightly and just coats the spoon. Do not boil or the custard will curdle. Strain into a large bowl; cool.

3 Add the yogurt, 350 g (12 oz) cranberries, grated rind of both limes and 30 ml (2 tbsp) lime juice. Blend in batches in a food processor until almost smooth.

4 Pour into a freezer container to a depth of about 5 cm (2 inches). Freeze for about 4 hours until mushy, then beat well to break down the ice crystals. Freeze again for at least 8 hours, until firm. (If using an ice-cream maker, churn mixture in the usual way.)

5 Place the remaining cranberries in a pan with the remaining sugar and orange juice. Place over a gentle heat until the sugar dissolves and the cranberries soften slightly. Pour into a bowl; cool. Cover and chill.

6 About 1½ hours before serving, transfer the ice cream to the refrigerator to soften. Serve scoops with the cranberries in syrup.

Freezing: suitable. Freeze the ice cream as directed. Pack and freeze the cranberries in syrup separately. When required, thaw at cool room temperature for about 4 hours.

Lime and Cranberry Ice at the back; Tuiles at the front

Tuiles

These biscuits have to be curled up around the handle of a wooden spoon the moment they come out of the oven, so don't try to cook too many at once. If allowed to cool, they will be difficult to roll.

45 cals per Tuile

2 egg whites
65 g (2½ oz) icing sugar, sieved
65 g (2½ oz) plain white flour
65 g (2½ oz) butter, melted
icing sugar, to dust

1 In a bowl, beat together the egg whites, the sieved icing sugar and the flour. Mix in the cooled butter.

2 Spoon two small spoonfuls of the mixture (about 7.5 ml (1½ tsp) each) onto a baking sheet lined with non-stick baking parchment. Smooth into oblongs about 4 x 20.5 cm (1½ x 8 inches).

3 Bake at 220°C (425°F) mark 7 for 3-4 minutes or until golden brown. Immediately remove from the paper using a palette knife and loosely roll each tuile around a wooden spoon handle; cool on a wire rack.

4 Repeat until all the mixture is used (makes about 24). Once cold, place the tuiles in a well-sealed rigid container with non-stick baking parchment between the layers. Store for up to a week.

5 Dust with icing sugar to serve.

Freezing: suitable. Layer with non-stick baking parchment in a rigid container. Thaw for about 15 minutes.

CHRISTMAS DRINKS PARTY MENU

Think pink at party time and serve these pretty canapés with sparkling wine to create an evening that everyone will remember!

Delicious and light as air to eat, the canapés are easy to prepare ahead of time, so that you can simply warm them through on the night. When planning the party, bear in mind that you should allow 8-10 bites per person, unless guests are going on to have dinner, in which case 5 canapés per person should suffice.

MENU FOR 20

All recipes make at least 20 bites

Honey Bacon Rolls
Mini BLTs
Pepper and Pesto Crostini
Spicy Prawns
Roast Beef and Potato Bites
Goats' Cheese Crostini
Salmon Millefeuilles

Blushing Dip
Cranberry Sparkler

COUNTDOWN

Up to four days ahead
Complete steps 1 and 2 of Salmon Millefeuilles. Store in an airtight container.

Two days ahead
Complete the Roast Beef and Potato Bites to the end of step 3. Store the flavoured cheese in the refrigerator. Cool, cover and chill the beef and potatoes separately. Complete steps 1 and 2 of Pepper and Pesto Crostini. Cool; cover and chill. Store the toasts in an airtight container. Make the toasts for Goats' Cheese Crostini; store in an airtight container.

The day before
Marinate the Spicy Prawns. Cover and chill. Complete the Honey Bacon Rolls to the end of step 2. Cover and chill. Complete the Mini BLTs to the end of step 2. Store the toasts in an airtight container. Make the Blushing Dip, cover and chill.

To serve at 8pm
6pm Complete the Spicy Prawns. Thinly slice the rare roast beef. Cover and chill.
6.30pm Warm the pastries for the Salmon Millefeuilles and complete as in steps 3 and 4. Warm the toasts for the BLTs and crostini and assemble.
7pm Reheat the potato slices for the Roast Beef and Potato Bites. Place, uncovered, on a baking sheet and place in a warm oven for 10 minutes to crisp up. Complete as in step 4.

Mini BLTs

Honey Bacon Rolls

Mini BLTs

80 cals per serving

10 small cherry tomatoes, about 50 g (2 oz)

1 Little Gem lettuce

75 g (3 oz) Parma ham

1 loaf sun-dried tomato bread

25 g (1 oz) butter

salt and pepper

30 ml (2 tbsp) mayonnaise

1 Halve the cherry tomatoes. Cut the lettuce into pieces about 4 cm (1½ inches) in length. Cut the Parma ham into 20 long strips.

2 Cut the bread into slices about 1 cm (½ inch) thick and spread with a little butter. Season with salt and pepper. Stamp out 40 rounds with a 4 cm (1½ inch) round cutter or cut into 4 cm (1½ inch) squares. Place, butter-side up, on a grill pan and toast under a hot grill for 1 minute or until golden. Repeat on the other side.

3 Spread mayonnaise on 20 of the toast rounds, place a piece of lettuce, then half a cherry tomato and a folded piece of ham on top, add lettuce and mayonnaise and another toast round; secure with a cocktail stick.

Freezing: not suitable

Honey Bacon Rolls

50 cals per serving

6 spring onions

175 g (6 oz) mixed vegetables, such as baby corn, carrot, mangetout

225 g (8 oz) rindless streaky bacon, about 12 slices

45 ml (3 tbsp) honey

30 ml (2 tbsp) soy sauce

1 Cut the spring onions and the mixed vegetables into thin matchsticks about 4 cm (1½ inches) long.

2 Stretch each rasher of bacon with the back of a knife and cut in half. Place a small pile of spring onions and vegetables at one end of the bacon rasher and roll up. Secure with a cocktail stick.

3 Place the rolls in a single layer in a roasting tin just large enough to hold them. Combine the honey and soy sauce and spoon over the bacon rolls. Cook at 200°C (400°F) mark 6 for 30-35 minutes or until golden, turning occasionally.

Freezing: not suitable

Pepper and Pesto Crostini

70 cals per serving

½ red pepper

½ orange pepper

25 g (1 oz) shallot

45 ml (3 tbsp) olive oil

salt and pepper

1 small loaf olive bread

1 garlic clove

30 ml (2 tbsp) red pesto

1 Deseed and finely dice the peppers. Peel and finely chop the shallot. Heat 15 ml (1 tbsp) olive oil in a frying pan and fry the peppers and shallot over a medium heat for 6 minutes or until just beginning to soften. Season with salt and pepper. Set aside.

2 Slice the bread into 1 cm (½ inch) thick slices. Cut the garlic in half and rub over the bread slices. Remove the crusts from the bread, cut into 3 cm (1¼ inch) squares and drizzle over the remaining olive oil. Toast under a hot grill for 1 minute on both sides or until golden.

3 Spread a little red pesto on each crostini and top with some of the warm pepper mixture.

Freezing: not suitable

Spicy Prawns

30 cals per serving

5 ml (1 tsp) hot chilli sauce

30 ml (2 tbsp) oil

juice of 1 lime

350 g (12 oz) cooked, peeled king prawns, with tails

1 Mix together the hot chilli sauce, oil and lime juice. Stir in the prawns, cover and marinate in a cool place for about 30 minutes.

2 Fry the marinated prawns quickly in a non-stick frying pan or wok. Serve with cocktail sticks to spear the prawns.

Freezing: not suitable

Roast Beef and Potato Bites

50 cals per serving

15-30 ml (1-2 tbsp) sun-dried tomato paste

100 g (3½ oz) full-fat soft cheese

15 ml (1 tbsp) creamed horseradish

salt and pepper

5 ml (1 tsp) mustard powder

15 ml (1 tbsp) soft brown sugar

25 g (1 oz) butter, softened

225 g (8 oz) beef fillet

350 g (12 oz) small new potatoes

15 ml (1 tbsp) olive oil

finely chopped fresh chives

1 Beat the tomato paste into the cheese with the horseradish until smooth. Season with salt and pepper. Cover and refrigerate until required.

2 Mix together the mustard powder, sugar and butter. Rub over the beef. Place in a small roasting tin. Cut the potatoes into 2 cm (¾ inch) thick slices, toss in the oil and place in a single layer in a shallow roasting tin.

3 Place the potatoes on the middle shelf and cook at 220°C (425°F) mark 7 for about 45 minutes until golden brown and tender. Turn once during cooking. Position the beef on the top shelf of the oven and cook for 25 minutes for rare, 35 minutes for medium.

4 Thinly slice the cooled beef and place a thin slice on each warm potato base. Spoon a little of the flavoured cheese on top and garnish with the chives.

Freezing: not suitable

Roast Beef and Potato Bites

Goats' Cheese Crostini

Goats' Cheese Crostini

40 cals per serving

1 thin baguette
225 g (8 oz) soft goats' cheese, crumbled
20 ml (4 tsp) tropical pepper (a mix of black and green peppers with pink berries), crushed

1 Cut the bread into thin slices and toast on both sides or bake at 180°C (350°F) mark 4 for about 10 minutes or until lightly coloured.

2 Top with the crumbled goats' cheese and the tropical pepper.

Freezing: not suitable

Salmon Millefeuilles

55 cals per serving

flour for dusting
225 g (8 oz) puff pastry
1 egg, beaten
30 ml (2 tbsp) gravadlax sauce
30 ml (2 tbsp) mayonnaise
45 ml (3 tbsp) mascarpone or low-fat soft cheese
50 g (2 oz) radish
50 g (2 oz) cucumber, about a 5 cm (2 inch) piece
125 g (4 oz) salmon gravadlax

1 Dust the work surface with flour and roll out the pastry 3 mm (⅛ inch) thick. Brush with beaten egg and stamp out 20 rounds, using a 4 cm (1½ inch) fluted cutter. Place on a baking sheet and chill for 30 minutes. Brush with beaten egg again.

2 Cook at 200°C (400°F) mark 6 for 15 minutes or until risen and golden brown. Leave to cool.

3 Mix the gravadlax sauce and mayonnaise with the cheese, then set aside. Thinly slice the radish. Deseed the cucumber and using a potato peeler, cut into thin strips. Cut the gravadlax into 2 cm (¾ inch) pieces.

4 To assemble: split each baked pastry round in two. Spread a little of the gravadlax-sauce mixture onto half the rounds. Place a piece of salmon on top, then a slice of radish and a piece of cucumber and continue layering. Top with a puff-pastry round.

Freezing: not suitable

Salmon Millefeuilles

Blushing Dip

Blushing Dip

60 cals per serving

2 passion fruit

150 ml (5 fl oz) double cream

150 ml (5 fl oz) Greek yogurt

15 ml (1 tbsp) caster sugar

pink food colouring

a selection of pink/red fruit, such as red grapes, figs, wedges of blood orange, segments of pink grapefruit, segments of red-skinned apple, lychees and strawberries, to serve

1 Halve the passion fruit and scoop out the pulp.
2 Lightly whip the double cream. Whip in the Greek yogurt, passion fruit pulp and caster sugar with 1-2 drops of pink food colouring. Cover and refrigerate.
3 Serve with the fruit for dipping.

Freezing: not suitable

Cranberry Sparkler

This inviting-looking punch is ideal to serve to guests who do not want an alcoholic drink.

54 cals per 150 ml (5 fl oz)

ice cubes

1 litre (1¾ pints) pink grapefruit juice

1 litre (1¾ pints) cranberry juice

2 litres (3½ pints) sparkling mineral water or old-fashioned pink lemonade

450 g (1 lb) fresh/frozen cranberries

1 Fill the glasses ⅓ full of ice cubes. Pour 50 ml (2 fl oz) grapefruit juice and 50 ml (2 fl oz) cranberry juice into each glass.
2 Top up with sparkling mineral water or lemonade and decorate with a few whole cranberries.

Freezing: not suitable

NEW YEAR'S EVE DINNER PARTY

Celebrate the start of the New Year with this stylish, mildly spicy buffet. Hand around the Vegetable Crisps with drinks instead of a starter, then follow with the main course.

MENU FOR 12

Vegetable Crisps
Tomato and Chilli Salsa

Caramelised Duckling
Spiced Rice and Lentils
Citrus Leeks with Sugar-Snap Peas

Golden Mascarpone Tarts

COUNTDOWN

The day before
Prepare the Vegetable Crisps, seal in airtight containers. Make the Tomato and Chilli Salsa, cover and refrigerate. Prepare the Caramelised Duckling to the end of step 3. Cool; refrigerate overnight. Prepare the Spiced Rice and Lentils without adding the parsley. Cool, cover and refrigerate. Prepare the citrus dressing for the vegetables, cover and refrigerate. Prepare the pastry cases for the Golden Mascarpone Tarts to the end of step 2. Cool, store in airtight containers. Prepare the vegetables, refrigerate in polythene bags.

On the day
To serve at 8pm
In the morning Complete step 3 of Golden Mascarpone Tarts and whisk together filling, but don't assemble. If serving the vegetables cold, complete and allow to cool at room temperature.

5.50pm Cook the Golden Mascarpone Tarts.
7pm Increase the oven temperature to 200°C (400°F) mark 6. Place the Spiced Rice and Lentils in a buttered dish, cover with foil and reheat in the oven. Remove the citrus dressing from the refrigerator. Arrange the Vegetable Crisps, keep covered in a basket. Pour the salsa into a serving dish and cover.
7.30pm Bring the Caramelised Duckling to the boil on the hob and place in the oven. If serving the vegetables warm, put them on to cook and keep warm.
7.50pm Stir the herbs and Parma ham into the casserole and adjust the seasoning. Stir the parsley into the rice. Keep warm.
8pm Serve. Put the loosely covered Golden Mascarpone Tarts back into a low oven to warm through.

Vegetable Crisps

About 130 cals per 25 g (1 oz)

900 g (2 lb) each parsnips and sweet potatoes

oil for deep-frying

salt

6 red chillies

paprika

Tomato and Chilli Salsa, to serve (see below)

1 Peel, then thinly slice the parsnips and sweet potatoes separately in a food processor. Keep completely covered in cold water until required.

2 In a deep-fat fryer, heat the oil to 170°C (325°F). Drain the parsnips and dry thoroughly on kitchen paper. Fry in small batches for 2-3 minutes, turning occasionally, until crisp and golden brown. Drain on kitchen paper to remove the excess oil; dust with salt.

3 Drop the chillies into the oil and fry the sweet potatoes with the chillies, as above. Drain on kitchen paper and dust with paprika.

4 Store separately in airtight containers for up to three days. To serve, pile the parsnip and sweet potato crisps into baskets and garnish with the deep-fried chillies. Serve with the Salsa.

Freezing: not suitable

Tomato and Chilli Salsa

40 cals per serving

900 g (2 lb) ripe tomatoes

6 anchovy fillets

10 ml (2 tsp) capers

1 small red chilli

15 g (½ oz) fresh white breadcrumbs

15 ml (1 tbsp) red wine vinegar

30 ml (2 tbsp) olive oil

5 ml (1 tsp) caster sugar

salt and pepper

1 Skin, deseed and finely chop the tomatoes. Roughly chop the anchovies and capers. Halve, deseed and finely chop the chilli.

2 Mix together with the next four ingredients. Season with salt and pepper to taste.

3 Blend half the mixture in a food processor until almost smooth. Stir into the remainder. Serve with the Vegetable Crisps.

Freezing: not suitable

Caramelised Duckling

It's important to brown the duckling well in hot oil in order to seal the meat and to give the casserole a good colour. Seal the duckling pieces in small batches to allow them to brown on all sides.

310 cals per serving

1.4 kg (3 lb) onions

about 120 ml (8 tbsp) olive oil

75 g (3 oz) soft light brown (muscovado) sugar

90 ml (6 tbsp) sherry vinegar

12 whole allspice berries

10 duckling breasts, about 1.8 kg (4 lb) total weight

50 g (2 oz) plain white flour

10 ml (2 tsp) paprika

salt and pepper

900 ml (1½ pints) chicken stock

20 ml (4 tsp) dry sherry

grated rind and juice of 1 lemon

10 ml (2 tsp) chopped fresh marjoram or 5 ml (1 tsp) dried

175 g (6 oz) Parma ham

flat-leaf parsley, to garnish

1 Peel, halve and slice the onions. Heat 30 ml (2 tbsp) oil in a large flameproof casserole. Add the onions and sauté, uncovered, for 20 minutes. Stir in the next three ingredients. Cook for about 5 minutes, until caramelised and a rich brown.

2 Meanwhile, skin the duckling and cut into bite-sized pieces. Mix the flour and paprika together, then season with salt and pepper. Coat the duckling in the flour.

3 Remove the onions and juices from the pan, rinse the pan and add 75 ml (5 tbsp) oil. Heat, then brown the duckling in batches, adding a little more oil if necessary. Drain on kitchen paper. Place all the duckling in the casserole with any remaining flour. Off the heat, stir in the stock with the onions, sherry, grated lemon rind and juice, and marjoram. Bring to the boil, cover and cook at 150°C (300°F) mark 2 for 50 minutes or until almost tender.

4 Lightly sauté the chopped Parma ham in 15 ml (1 tbsp) oil for 3-4 minutes. Stir into the duckling. Cover and cook for a further 10 minutes or until the duckling is tender. Season and garnish with flat-leaf parsley.

Freezing: suitable at the end of step 3, without adding the herbs. Thaw overnight at cool room temperature. Bring to the boil on the hob then reheat at 150°C (300°F) mark 2 for 50 minutes-1 hour. Stir in the herbs and sautéed Parma ham and a little more stock, if necessary, 10 minutes before serving.

Spiced Rice and Lentils

230 cals per serving

225 g (8 oz) onions

45 ml (3 tbsp) olive oil

3 bay leaves

1 cinnamon stick

5 whole green cardamoms, split

5 ml (1 tsp) fennel seeds

225 g (8 oz) whole green lentils

50 g (2 oz) wild rice

600 ml (1 pint) light stock

salt and pepper

400 g (14 oz) long-grain white rice

45 ml (3 tbsp) chopped fresh parsley

1 Peel and finely chop the onions. Heat the oil in a large saucepan. Sauté the onions with the next four ingredients for 3-4 minutes until the mixture starts to turn brown.

2 Add the next three ingredients with 1.4 litres (2½ pints) water and 1.25 ml (¼ tsp) salt. Bring to the boil, cover and simmer gently for 15 minutes.

3 Add the white rice, bring back to the boil, cover and simmer for a further 10 minutes. Remove the lid and cook for a further 5 minutes, stirring occasionally.

4 Drain, remove the cinnamon stick and bay leaves. Stir in the parsley; season with salt and pepper and serve.

Freezing: not suitable

Citrus Leeks with Sugar-Snap Peas

150 cals per serving

1.4 kg (3 lb) trimmed leeks

900 g (2 lb) sugar-snap peas or mangetouts

45-60 ml (3-4 tbsp) olive oil

salt and pepper

DRESSING

100 ml (4 fl oz) olive oil

25 ml (1 fl oz) balsamic vinegar

5 ml (1 tsp) soft light brown sugar

15-30 ml (1-2 tbsp) lemon juice

5 ml (1 tsp) Dijon mustard

grated rind and juice of 1 orange

1 Wash and cut the leeks into 1 cm (½ inch) slices. Top and tail the sugar-snap peas.

2 Heat the oil in a large sauté pan. Add the leeks and sauté gently for 5-6 minutes or until just tender. Cook the sugar-snap peas in boiling, salted water for 5 minutes. Drain, then mix with the leeks.

3 Mix together all the dressing ingredients, then season with salt and pepper. Stir into the hot vegetables and serve hot or cold.

Freezing: not suitable

Golden Mascarpone Tarts

Italian mascarpone cheese is rich and creamy. If you can't find it, beat together 200 g (7 oz) full-fat soft cheese with 150 ml (5 fl oz) single cream. The mixture will set a little firmer, but will be just as delicious. If you are not keen on cooked bananas, use another pear instead.

450 cals per serving

275 g (10 oz) plain white flour

175 g (6 oz) caster sugar

150 g (5 oz) unsalted butter

450 g (1 lb) pears

2 bananas

350 g (12 oz) fresh dates

40 g (1½ oz) butter

350 g (12 oz) mascarpone cheese

4 eggs, size 3

30 ml (2 tbsp) rum

2.5 ml (½ tsp) vanilla essence

about 75 ml (5 tbsp) soft dark brown sugar

single cream, to accompany

1 Mix together the flour and 125 g (4 oz) caster sugar. Rub in the unsalted butter until the mixture resembles breadcrumbs. Stir in 60-75 ml (4-5 tbsp) water then gently knead the dough until smooth. Wrap and chill for 30 minutes.

2 Use the dough to line two 34 x 11.5 cm (13½ x 4½ inch) loose-based, fluted tranche tins. Chill the pastry cases well. Prick the bases well, then line the pastry cases with greaseproof paper and baking beans. Bake at 200°C (400°F) mark 6 for about 10 minutes, until just set. Remove the baking beans and paper and return the pastry cases to the oven for a further 10 minutes until they are light golden.

3 Peel, quarter and core the pears; slice the banana; halve and stone the dates. Melt the butter in a large, heavy-based sauté pan, stir in the pears and dates, sauté for 3-4 minutes until beginning to soften. Add the banana and cook for a further 1 minute.

4 Divide the fruit between the tranche tins. Whisk together the next four ingredients with the remaining caster sugar until smooth, then spoon over the fruit to cover. Sprinkle 30 ml (2 tbsp) dark brown sugar over each tin.

5 Bake at 170°C (325°F) mark 3 for about 35 minutes or until just set. Sprinkle over a little more soft dark brown sugar and flash under a hot grill to caramelise the sugar. Serve warm with single cream.

Freezing: suitable at the end of step 2. Thaw overnight at cool room temperature.

Golden Mascarpone Tarts

canapés

Filo Moneybags

For an attractive finishing touch, tie a chive around the neck of each moneybag.

To make in advance, deep-fry the moneybags in the morning, then cool and refrigerate. Reheat, uncovered, on a baking sheet at 200°C (400°F) mark 6 for 10-15 minutes.

Preparation time: about 30 minutes
Cooking time: 30 minutes
125 cals per moneybag
Makes about 35

125 g (4 oz) butter

60 ml (4 tbsp) oil, plus oil for deep-frying

250 g (9 oz) filo pastry

SPINACH AND BLUE CHEESE FILLING

1 small onion

225 g (8 oz) blue cheese, such as Stilton

50 g (2 oz) frozen leaf spinach, thawed

2 garlic cloves

25 g (1 oz) butter

150 ml (5 fl oz) double cream

salt and pepper

1 To make the filling, peel and chop the onion. Cut the cheese into small cubes. Squeeze the spinach to remove excess liquid; finely chop.

2 Fry the onion and the crushed garlic in the butter until soft. Add the spinach and cream. Bubble and reduce until nearly dry. Cool, then blend in the cheese and season with salt and pepper. Cover and chill.

3 To assemble the moneybags, melt 125 g (4 oz) butter and add 60 ml (4 tbsp) oil. Cut the pastry into 9 cm (3½ inch) squares; cover with cling film. Brush three squares with butter. Place one on top of the other to form a 12-point star.

4 Place a teaspoonful of the filling in the pastry centre, then draw up the edges. Pinch and seal into shape. Repeat making moneybags in this way with the remaining filling and pastry.

5 Deep-fry the parcels in batches of 10 for 3 minutes or until golden. Drain and serve.

Freezing: suitable, at the end of step 5. Reheat, uncovered on a baking sheet, at 200°C (400°F) mark 6 for 15-20 minutes.

VARIATION

For a prawn and spring onion filling, chop 225 g (8 oz) cooked, peeled prawns and combine with 6 finely chopped spring onions and 1 chopped garlic clove. Peel and grate a 1 cm (½ inch) piece fresh root ginger and mix into the prawn mixture with 30 ml (2 tbsp) chopped fresh coriander and 40 g (1½ oz) melted butter. Use as for step 4 of the recipe and serve with a chilli dip.

Turkey and Chestnut Tarts

The tarts can be cooked and stored in an airtight container up to 2 days ahead. Make the filling without the cranberry sauce the day before; cover and chill. On the day, complete the sauce, assemble the tarts and serve within 10 minutes.

Preparation time: 10 minutes
Cooking time: 5 minutes
45 cals per tart
Makes 30

125 g (4 oz) filo pastry

50 g (2 oz) butter, melted

75 g (3 oz) cooked turkey breast

30 ml (2 tbsp) sunflower oil

10 ml (2 tsp) wine vinegar

10 ml (2 tsp) Dijon mustard

150 g (5 oz) vacuum-packed or canned chestnuts

10 ml (2 tsp) chopped fresh thyme or pinch dried

15 ml (1 tbsp) cranberry sauce

salt and pepper

herb sprigs, to garnish

1 Brush the sheets of filo pastry lightly with butter. Sandwich three on top of each other and cut into 5 cm (2 inch) squares. Keep covered with cling film. Press into non-stick mini-muffin tins and cook in batches at 200°C (400°F) mark 6 for 5 minutes or until golden and crisp. Cool.

2 Cut the turkey into fine strips. In a bowl, whisk together

Mini Yorkshires, Turkey and Chestnut Tarts and Filo Moneybags

the sunflower oil, wine vinegar and mustard.

3 Chop the chestnuts and stir into the dressing with the turkey, thyme, cranberry sauce and seasoning.

4 Fill the tart cases with the mixture and garnish with a herb sprig.

Freezing: not suitable

Mini Yorkshires

The ideal tins for Mini Yorkshires are non-stick mini-muffin tins. The Yorkshires can be made up to 2 days ahead and stored in an airtight container; warm them in a moderate oven before filling and serving.

Preparation time: 10 minutes
Cooking time: 40 minutes
75 cals each
Makes about 36

1 bunch watercress, about 75 g (3 oz)

1 egg

125 g (4 oz) plain white flour

25 ml (5 tsp) English mustard powder

300 ml (10 fl oz) milk

oil

salt and pepper

15 ml (1 tbsp) soft brown sugar

25 g (1 oz) butter, softened

350 g (12 oz) beef fillet

150 ml (5 fl oz) double cream

45 ml (3 tbsp) horseradish sauce

1 Reserve 30 small watercress sprigs in the refrigerator for garnishing. Blend the remainder with the egg, flour, 10 ml (2 tsp) mustard powder, milk and 30 ml (2 tbsp) oil until smooth. Season well with salt and pepper.
2 Mix together the remaining mustard with the sugar and butter. Rub over the beef and cook at 220°C (425°F) mark 7 for 20 minutes for rare, 30 minutes for medium; cool.
3 Drizzle oil in each cup of a mini-muffin tin and heat in the oven. Fill the cups with 15 ml (1 tbsp) batter and cook at 220°C (425°F) mark 7 for 15-20 minutes or until risen and pale brown. Cool. (Makes about three batches of 12.)
4 Lightly whip the cream with the horseradish sauce. Season well. Cut the beef into fine strips.
5 Hollow out the puddings. Put a teaspoonful of horseradish cream in each base, then fill with a little beef. Garnish with watercress sprigs.

Freezing: suitable for the unfilled Mini Yorkshires. Thaw and warm at 180°C (350°F) mark 4 for 10 minutes.

Mini Fishcakes with Hollandaise Dip

Delicious little fishcakes served with a watercress-flavoured dip make moreish bites to serve with drinks.

To prepare the fishcakes ahead, cook them in the morning, cool, cover and chill. Reheat uncovered at 200°C (400°F) mark 6 for 10 minutes and complete as directed.

Preparation time: 10 minutes
Cooking time: 20 minutes
160 cals per fishcake
Makes 30

125 g (4 oz) each salmon and smoked haddock fillet, skinned

2 large potatoes, about 400 g (14 oz)

150 g (5 oz) butter

salt and pepper

15 ml (1 tbsp) each chopped fresh parsley, dill and chives, or 5 ml (1 tsp) dried dill weed

3 eggs

50 g (2 oz) plain white flour

125 g (4 oz) fresh white breadcrumbs

45 ml (3 tbsp) oil

HOLLANDAISE DIP
250 ml (9 fl oz) jar hollandaise sauce

30 ml (2 tbsp) finely chopped watercress

1 Poach the salmon and haddock in a covered pan of gently simmering water for about 10 minutes or until cooked through. Strain, cool and flake the fish.
2 Meanwhile, boil the potatoes, then drain and mash. Add 50 g (2 oz) butter and season well with salt and pepper. Leave to cool. Add the flaked fish, herbs and one beaten egg.
3 Turn out the mixture onto a well-floured work surface and flatten the mixture with your hand until it is about 2 cm (¾ inch) thick. Stamp out 30 fishcakes with a 3 cm (1¼ inch) round cutter. Chill for 1 hour.
4 Beat together the remaining eggs. Dip the fishcakes first in flour, then beaten egg and finally breadcrumbs.

Mini Fishcakes with Hollandaise Dip

5 Fry the fishcakes in batches in the oil and remaining butter for 2 minutes on each side or until golden brown. Drain thoroughly on kitchen paper.

6 To make the dip, warm the hollandaise sauce through, according to the bottle instructions. Stir in the chopped watercress and serve with the fishcakes.

Freezing: suitable at the end of step 5. Thaw overnight at cool room temperature. Reheat, uncovered, at 200°C (400°F) mark 6 for 10 minutes.

and line 60 mini tartlet tins. Prick the bases well and chill for 30 minutes. Cook at 200°C (400°F) mark 6 for 10 minutes or until the tarts are golden.

3 Meanwhile, roughly chop the shellfish. Whisk together the remaining egg, saffron, cream and chives, then season with salt and pepper. Fill each pastry case with some shellfish, topped with a teaspoonful of the saffron mixture. Cook for 5-10 minutes at 200°C (400°F) mark 6 Garnish with chives and serve immediately.

Freezing: suitable, without garnish. Thaw overnight at cool room temperature. Reheat at 200°C (400°F) mark 6 for 5-10 minutes or until hot; garnish.

Shellfish and Saffron Tarts

Shellfish and Saffron Tarts

Preparation time: 50 minutes, plus chilling
Cooking time: 20 minutes
65 cals per canapé
Makes 60

350 g (12 oz) plain flour

175 g (6 oz) butter

75 g (3 oz) freshly grated Parmesan cheese

3 eggs

225 g (8 oz) cooked prawns or white crabmeat

pinch of saffron strands

150 ml (5 fl oz) double cream

75 ml (3 tbsp) chopped fresh chives

salt and pepper

fresh chives, to garnish

1 To make the pastry, process the flour, butter and cheese until the mixture resembles fine crumbs. Add two lightly beaten eggs and 45 ml (3 tbsp) iced water; pulse until the crumbs come together to form a dough. Wrap in cling film and chill for 30 minutes.

2 Roll out the pastry thinly on a lightly floured work surface. Stamp out rounds with a 5 cm (2 inch) plain cutter

Mozzarella and Basil Choux

Preparation time: 10 minutes
Cooking time: 30 minutes
45 cals per canapé
Makes about 50

CHOUX PASTRY

3 eggs

125 g (4 oz) mozzarella cheese

75 g (3 oz) butter

125 g (4 oz) plain flour

10 basil leaves, roughly chopped

salt and pepper

FILLING

175 g (6 oz) sun-dried tomatoes

125 g (4 oz) soft garlic cheese

1 large bunch basil

30-45 ml (2-3 tbsp) milk (optional)

30 ml (2 tbsp) freshly grated Parmesan cheese

1 To make the choux pastry, lightly beat the eggs, then dice the mozzarella cheese.

2 Pour 200 ml (7 fl oz) cold water into a medium-sized saucepan, add the butter and melt over a low heat. Increase the heat and bring to a rolling boil. Take off the heat and immediately add all the flour. Mix to a smooth paste. Return to the heat to dry a little, then cool until tepid. Slowly add the eggs, beating well between each addition. Add the mozzarella and basil, then season well with salt and pepper. Spoon the mixture in 1 cm (½ inch) rounds onto a non-stick baking tray. Cook at 200°C (400°F) mark 6 for 15 minutes or until puffed and golden. Cool.

3 For the filling, blend the sun-dried tomatoes, cheese and basil in a food processor until smooth. Add enough milk to bring to a soft consistency. Season well. Make a slit in the choux, then fill with the tomato mixture.

4 Place the choux on a baking tray, sprinkle with Parmesan cheese and reheat at 200°C (400°F) mark 6 for 3-5 minutes.

Freezing: suitable at the end of step 3. Thaw at cool room temperature overnight. Reheat at 200°C (400°F) mark 6 for 7-10 minutes.

Rosti with Cranberry and Onion Confit

Rosti with Cranberry and Onion Confit

Preparation time: 20 minutes
Cooking time: 50 minutes
30 cals per canapé
Makes about 50

350 g (12 oz) each potatoes and parsnips

4 eggs

salt and pepper

75 g (3 oz) onion

45-60 ml (3-4 tbsp) oil for frying

225 g (8 oz) cranberries

150 ml (5 fl oz) orange juice

15 ml (1 tbsp) caster sugar

175 g (6 oz) soft goats' cheese

flat-leaf parsley, to garnish

1 Peel the potatoes and parsnips, then grate them coarsely into a large bowl and cover with cold water. Lightly beat the eggs and season well with salt and pepper.

2 Peel and finely chop the onion. Heat 15 ml (1 tbsp) of the oil in a heavy-based pan, add the onion and cook, stirring, for 10 minutes or until golden and soft. Add the cranberries, orange juice and sugar. Bring to the boil, then simmer, uncovered, for 30 minutes or until reduced. Season with salt and pepper to taste; cool.

3 Drain the potato mixture, dry it on kitchen paper, then stir in the beaten eggs. Heat the remaining 30-45 ml (2-3 tbsp) oil in a large, heavy-based, non-stick frying pan. Add teaspoonfuls of the mixture; cook in batches for 2-3 minutes on each side or until golden and crisp. Drain on kitchen paper.

4 Leave to cool slightly, then spread each rosti with goats' cheese and top with a spoonful of the confit. Garnish with parsley.

Freezing: suitable. Open-freeze the rosti at the end of step 3. Store the confit in an airtight container in the refrigerator for up to a week. Reheat frozen rosti on a baking sheet, at 200°C (400°F) mark 6 for 15 minutes. Cool slightly and complete recipe.

Savoury Stars

1 In a food processor, blend the flour, cheese, butter, salt and cayenne pepper until the pastry forms a ball shape. Knead lightly, wrap in cling film and chill for about 10 minutes.

2 Meanwhile, finely chop the tomatoes, nuts and olives.

3 Roll out the pastry on a floured work surface until it is about 5 mm (¼ inch) thick. Brush with beaten egg, then sprinkle on an even layer of tomato, nuts and olives. Fold the pastry into a neat parcel shape to enclose the filling completely.

4 Roll out the parcel of pastry to a 1 cm (½ inch) thickness. Use Christmas tree, star and moon cutters to stamp out shapes, then place on baking sheets. Brush lightly with beaten egg and sprinkle on poppy, caraway or sesame seeds. Chill the pastry shapes for about 20 minutes.

5 Bake at 180°C (350°F) mark 4 for about 15-20 minutes or until well browned. Leave on the baking sheets for about 5 minutes before removing to a cooling rack.

Freezing: suitable. Thaw at cool room temperature for about 1 hour.

VARIATIONS

Omit the tomatoes, pistachio nuts and olives and replace with half a can of anchovy fillets soaked in milk for 30 minutes, then drained and finely chopped, or with freshly chopped herbs.

Savoury Stars

These stars work well when served with crunchy vegetables filled with cream cheese to provide a delicious contrast in taste and texture.

Preparation time: 40 minutes, plus chilling
Cooking time: 20 minutes
35 cals per star
Makes about 40

75 g (3 oz) plain white flour

75 g (3 oz) freshly grated Parmesan cheese

75 g (3 oz) butter

2.5 ml (½ tsp) salt

2.5 ml (½ tsp) cayenne pepper

25 g (1 oz) sun-dried tomatoes

25 g (1 oz) pistachio nuts

25 g (1 oz) pitted black olives

1 beaten egg, to glaze

5 ml (1 tsp) poppy seeds, caraway seeds or sesame seeds

Golden Bites

The uncooked shapes can be made up to two days ahead if stored in the refrigerator; cook for 25 minutes on the day.

Preparation time: 30 minutes, plus chilling
Cooking time: 20 minutes
55 cals per bite
Makes about 80

350 g (12 oz) plain flour

175 g (6 oz) butter

75 g (3 oz) freshly grated Parmesan cheese

pinch of cayenne pepper

pinch of mustard powder

2 egg yolks

225 g (8 oz) rindless streaky bacon

225 g (8 oz) soft rindless goats' cheese

ground black pepper

beaten egg, to glaze

1 Place the first five ingredients in a food processor and blend for 1 minute or until the mixture resembles fine breadcrumbs.

2 Add the egg yolks mixed with 90 ml (6 tbsp) water. Blend until the mixture just comes together. Divide into two balls, wrap and chill for 30 minutes.

3 Meanwhile, grill the bacon, drain and chop finely. Combine the bacon with the cheese. Season with pepper.

4 Roll the pastry to 3 mm (⅛ inch) thick. Cut out 6.5 cm (2 ½ inch) rounds and brush the edges with egg. Place 2.5 ml (½ tsp) filling on one side of each round, then fold over like a tiny pasty. Seal the edges. Place on a baking sheet and chill for at least 1 hour.

5 Brush the bites with egg glaze. Cook at 200°C (400°F) mark 6 for 20 minutes or until golden brown.

Freezing: suitable at the end of step 4. Reheat from frozen for 10-12 minutes at 200°C (400°F) mark 6.

Mini Wholemeal Blinis

To prepare in advance, complete the blinis and crème fraîche mixture up to one day ahead and refrigerate separately. Assemble up to 3 hours in advance and chill until required.

Preparation time: 30 minutes, plus rising time
Cooking time: 30 minutes
60 cals per blini
Makes about 100

175 ml (6 fl oz) milk

40 g (1½ oz) butter

2 eggs

125 g (4 oz) plain flour

50 g (2 oz) wholemeal flour

7.5 ml (1½ tsp) easy-blend dried yeast

5 ml (1 tsp) caster sugar

2.5 ml (½ tsp) salt

30 ml (2 tbsp) chopped chives

oil for frying

TOPPING

8 spring onions

450 g (1 lb) crème fraîche or soured cream

pepper

350 g (12 oz) smoked salmon

350 g (12 oz) cooked prawns

175 g (6 oz) salmon roe

dill sprigs or chives to garnish

1 Heat the milk with the butter until the butter melts. Set aside to cool a little. Separate the eggs.

2 Place the flours, yeast, sugar and salt in a food processor and work for for 30 seconds. With the machine running, add the warm milk mixture, then the egg yolks. Pour into a bowl, cover with cling film and leave to rise in a warm place for 45 minutes or until doubled in size.

3 Whisk the egg whites until stiff but not dry, then fold into the yeast batter with the chives.

4 Brush a little oil over a non-stick frying pan and heat through. Drop teaspoonfuls of the mixture into the pan and cook for 40 seconds on both sides or until golden; set aside.

5 To make the topping, finely chop the spring onions (including tops). Stir into the crème fraîche and season with pepper. Thinly shred the salmon.

6 Spoon a little of the crème fraîche mixture onto the blinis. Top half the blinis with salmon shreds and the other half with prawns. Add a little salmon roe to each, season with pepper and garnish with fresh sprigs of dill or chives.

Freezing: suitable, blinis only without topping. Thaw for 2-3 hours at cool room temperature. Assemble up to 3 hours before serving.

Aromatic Duck Bites

The mixture of crunchy vegetables and moist roast duck makes an excellent combination.

Preparation time: 20 minutes, plus overnight marinating, cooling and chilling
Cooking time: 20 minutes
70 cals per bite
Makes 15

6 star anise

2.5 cm (1 inch) root ginger, finely chopped

150 ml (¼ pint) rice wine or sherry

60 ml (4 tbsp) dark soy sauce

1 large duck breast, about 225 g (8 oz)

10 ml (2 level tsp) sea salt flakes

ground black pepper

2 spring onions, finely chopped

75 g (3 oz) pear, unpeeled and finely chopped

30 ml (2 tbsp) plum sauce

30 ml (2 level tbsp) chopped fresh coriander

½ cucumber, cut into 15 x 1 cm (½ inch) slices

spring onion curls, to garnish

1 In a small bowl, mix together the star anise, ginger, rice wine and soy sauce. Score the skin on the duck breast and place in the marinade. Cover; chill overnight.

2 Remove the duck from the marinade and rub the skin with the salt and pepper. Heat a heavy-based frying pan and cook the duck, skin-side down, for 5 minutes. Turn the duck over and cook for a further 5 minutes.

3 Place the duck in a small roasting tin and cook, skin-up, at 200°C (400°F) mark 6 for 10 minutes. Cool.

4 In a bowl, mix together the spring onions, pear, plum sauce and coriander. Cover and chill.

5 Cut the duck thinly and place one piece on a slice of cucumber. Top with a spoonful of the plum sauce mixture and garnish with spring onion curls.

Freezing: not suitable

SPRING ONION CURLS
Finely slice spring onions into 9 cm (3½ inch) strips. Place in a bowl of cold water and chill for at least 4 hours.

Lingonberry and Camembert Tartlets

Lingonberry – the Swedish relative of the cranberry – makes a good sauce that marries well with cheese. You can substitute cranberry sauce if you prefer.

Preparation time: 30 minutes
Cooking time: 6 minutes
160 cals per tart
Makes 15

4 sheets of filo pastry

100 g (3½ oz) butter, melted

100 g (3½ oz) ripe Camembert or Brie, cut into 15 pieces

125 g (4 oz) wild lingonberry sauce or cranberry sauce

1 Using a sharp knife, cut each pastry sheet into 15 x 5 cm (2 inch) squares. (When working with filo, it's important to keep the pastry covered with a damp cloth while it's waiting to be used, otherwise it will dry out.)

2 Place a filo pastry square on a board, brush with melted butter, then place another filo square on top at an angle and brush again with butter. Continue with two more squares, brushing each with butter and turning at an angle until you have created a star effect. Gently press the filo into a small cocktail tart tin. Repeat the process to make 14 more tarts.

3 Place a piece of Camembert or Brie into each of the filo tartlets. Arrange the tartlets on a baking sheet and cook in the oven at 200°C (400°F) mark 6 for 5-6 minutes or until the filo is golden brown and the cheese has melted.

4 Remove the tartlets from the oven and place on a serving plate. Spoon one heaped teaspoon of the lingonberry or cranberry sauce on top of each tartlet, then serve immediately.

Freezing: not suitable

starters

Christmas Broth

Pigeon has been used to flavour this broth – an ideal start to a Christmas feast – but you can make it with pheasant or grouse if you prefer.

Preparation time: 25 minutes
Cooking time: 1½ hours
240 cals per serving
Serves 6

2 wood pigeons, each about 450 g (1 lb)

125 g (4 oz) each onions, celery and carrot

125 g (4 oz) rindless smoked back bacon

3 garlic cloves

45 ml (3 tbsp) oil

150 ml (5 fl oz) each port and red wine

1.7 litres (3 pints) chicken stock

2 sprigs thyme

2 bay leaves

5 ml (1 tsp) redcurrant jelly

salt and pepper

175 g (6 oz) cooked, vacuum-packed chestnuts

croûtons, to serve

chopped flat-leaf parsley, to garnish

Christmas Broth

1 Cut the breasts off the pigeons and remove the skin. Cut the flesh into strips 4 cm (1½ inches) long and 5 mm (¼ inch) wide, cover and set aside. Cut up the pigeon carcasses roughly. Cut the vegetables and bacon into 1 cm (½ inch) dice. Peel and crush the garlic.

2 Heat the oil and cook the carcasses over a high heat for 10 minutes until very brown. Add the vegetables, bacon and crushed garlic; cook, stirring, for 10 minutes, or until the vegetables are soft. Add the port and red wine; bring to the boil and bubble until reduced by half. Stir in the stock, herbs and jelly. Bring back to the boil and simmer gently, uncovered, for 1 hour.

3 Remove the bones and herbs; season the broth with salt and pepper.

4 Bring the broth back to the boil, then reduce to a simmer. Roughly chop the chestnuts and add with the pigeon strips. Bring to the boil, then simmer for 1-2 minutes to cook. Serve with croûtons, garnished with parsley.

Freezing: suitable at the end of step 3. Freeze pigeon strips separately. Thaw overnight at cool room temperature, then complete step 4.

Mushroom and Artichoke Soup with Walnuts

It is essential that the mushrooms impart their full flavour to the stock. Before straining the stock, check that they are quite tasteless.

Preparation time: 20 minutes, plus soaking
Cooking time: 1½ hours
250 cals per serving
Serves 4

15 g (½ oz) dried ceps
150 ml (5 fl oz) boiling water
1 small onion

450 g (1 lb) chestnut mushrooms
25 g (1 oz) butter
15 ml (1 tbsp) chopped fresh thyme
75 ml (3 fl oz) dry sherry
1.2 litres (2 pints) vegetable stock
450 g (1 lb) Jerusalem artichokes
1 garlic clove
30 ml (2 tbsp) walnut oil
salt and pepper
25 g (1 oz) walnuts, chopped and toasted
extra walnut oil, to serve
thyme sprigs, to garnish

1 Put the dried ceps into a bowl, pour over the boiling water and soak for 30 minutes. Drain, reserving the liquid.

2 Peel and chop the onion; chop the mushrooms. Melt the butter in a saucepan, add the onion and thyme and fry gently for 10 minutes until soft but not browned. Increase the heat, add the chestnut mushrooms and ceps and stir-fry for 2 minutes. Add the sherry and boil rapidly until well reduced.

3 Add the vegetable stock and reserved cep stock and bring to the boil. Cover and simmer gently for 20 minutes until the stock is rich tasting.

4 Meanwhile, peel and dice the artichokes. Peel and chop the garlic. Heat the oil in a large pan, add the artichokes and garlic and fry for 10 minutes, stirring, until evenly browned.

5 Strain the mushroom liquid through a fine sieve and add to the artichokes. Bring to the boil, cover and simmer for 35-40 minutes until the artichokes are cooked. Transfer to a blender or food processor and purée until very smooth.

6 Return the soup to the pan and heat gently for 5 minutes. Season with salt and pepper. Scatter the toasted nuts over the soup and drizzle with walnut oil. Serve at once, garnished with thyme.

Freezing: suitable at the end of step 6, without the garnish. Thaw overnight at cool room temperature, then reheat.

VARIATION
Stir 150 ml (5 fl oz) single cream into the puréed artichokes at the end of step 5. Finish as above.

Ham and Herb Terrine

This terrine makes a very good starter or buffet dish as it keeps well for a few days in the refrigerator – the flavour even improves with keeping!

Preparation time: 35 minutes, plus overnight soaking
Cooking time: about 1½ hours
450-340 cals per serving
Serves 6-8

1.1 kg (2½ lb) piece unsmoked gammon

1 onion

1 carrot

1 leek

1 celery stick

1 bouquet garni

6 black peppercorns

300 ml (10 fl oz) dry white wine

6 good thin slices of Parma ham or prosciutto, plus an extra 125 g (4 oz)

salt and pepper

30 ml (2 tbsp) wholegrain mustard

25 g (1 oz) powdered gelatine

90 ml (6 tbsp) chopped mixed fresh herbs (parsley, tarragon, chives)

salad leaves, to garnish

1 Cover the ham with cold water and leave to soak overnight to draw out excess salt.

2 Pour off the water and rinse the ham. Place in a pan. Peel the onion and carrot; trim and clean the leek. Add these vegetables to the pan with the celery, bouquet garni, peppercorns, wine and enough water to cover. Slowly bring to the boil, skim, then simmer very gently for 1½ hours or until the ham is very tender. Keep skimming throughout cooking to ensure a clear stock. Allow to cool for 10 minutes.

3 Meanwhile, line a 1.1 litre (2 pint) mould with overlapping slices of Parma ham. Shred the 125 g (4 oz) Parma ham.

4 Take the meat out of the liquid. Cut off and discard the fat and skin. Using two forks, tear the meat into large chunks and mix with the Parma ham. Pile all the meat roughly into the lined mould.

5 Strain the stock through a fine sieve or through a sieve lined with kitchen paper into a measuring jug – you should have at least 900 ml (1½ pints). Leave to cool, then chill – the fat will rise to the surface and set on top.

6 Remove the layer of fat and pour the stock into a saucepan. Boil rapidly to reduce to 900 ml (1½ pints) if necessary. Season the stock with salt and pepper to taste. Stir in the mustard. Sprinkle the gelatine over the surface of the hot stock and stir in until dissolved. Remove from the heat and stir in the chopped herbs. Cool until syrupy, then pour sufficient stock over the ham in the terrine to cover it. Tap the terrine on the surface to dislodge any trapped air bubbles. Chill for at least 2 hours until set.

7 To unmould, dip briefly in warm water and turn out onto a serving dish. Cut into thick slices and garnish with salad leaves.

Freezing: not suitable

Salmon and Tarragon Mousse

A tangy tomato and fennel salsa adds a piquant flavour to this smooth salmon and soft-cheese starter. For easy entertaining, the mousses can be made up to one day in advance, but cook them for 15 minutes only.

Preparation time: 1 hour 20 minutes, plus chilling
Cooking time: 20 minutes
340 cals per serving
Serves 10

grated rind and juice of 1 lemon

pinch of sugar

salt and pepper

90 ml (6 tbsp) extra virgin olive oil

275 g (10 oz) skinned and boned salmon fillet

450 g (1 lb) thinly sliced smoked salmon

2 eggs

cayenne pepper

225 ml (8 fl oz) double cream

30 ml (2 tbsp) chopped, fresh tarragon or 5 ml (1 tsp) dried

Salmon and Tarragon Mousse

125 g (4 oz) full-fat soft cheese

4 tomatoes

1 small bulb fennel

tarragon sprigs, to garnish (optional)

1 In a small bowl, combine a little lemon rind with 20 ml (4 tsp) lemon juice, sugar, salt, pepper and oil. Cover and set aside.

2 Roughly chop the salmon and 125 g (4 oz) smoked salmon. Place in a food processor or blender and process until smooth. While the machine is still running, add the eggs, one at a time. Transfer the mixture to a bowl, then beat in the remaining grated lemon rind and season with salt, pepper and a pinch of cayenne pepper. Cover and chill for at least 30 minutes.

3 Using a wooden spoon, gradually beat 200 ml (7 fl oz) cream into the salmon mixture, one tablespoonful at a time. Cover and chill for another 30 minutes.

4 In a small bowl, beat together the tarragon, cheese and remaining cream until smooth. Season, cover and chill for 30 minutes.

5 Line ten 100 ml (4 fl oz) ramekins with half the remaining smoked salmon – cut discs of smoked salmon to fit the bases and strips to line the sides. Half-fill the ramekins with salmon mousse. Place a teaspoon of tarragon cheese in the middle of each ramekin, then top with the remaining mousse. Cover with the remaining smoked salmon. Place the ramekins in a roasting tin and chill for 30 minutes.

6 Pour enough boiling water into the roasting tin to come halfway up the sides of the ramekins, then cover with foil. Cook at 170°C (325°F) mark 3 for 20 minutes or until the mousses are just set and firm to the touch. Remove from the roasting tin and leave to cool.

7 Meanwhile, skin, quarter and deseed the tomatoes. Cut the flesh into fine strips. Trim the fennel, reserving the feathery fronds. Halve lengthways, then cut into fine strips and toss with the tomato.

8 To serve, turn the mousses out onto plates. Toss the tomato and fennel salsa in the reserved lemon dressing and spoon around the mousses. Garnish with sprigs of tarragon or the reserved fennel fronds.

Freezing: suitable. Complete up to the end of step 6, cooking the mousses for 15 minutes only. Thaw at cool room temperature overnight. Complete from step 7.

Potted Pheasant with Thyme and Gin

Potted Pheasant with Thyme and Gin

Adding gin to this dish, along with the dry white wine, gives a subtle yet delicious juniper flavour to this unusual starter.

Preparation time: 25 minutes, plus chilling
Cooking time: 3 hours
385-310 cals per serving
Serves 8-10

2 pheasants or guinea fowl

250 g (9 oz) unsalted butter

8 garlic cloves

5 ml (1 tsp) grated nutmeg

8 black peppercorns

300 ml (10 fl oz) dry white wine

150 ml (5 fl oz) gin

handful fresh thyme or 15 ml (1 tbsp) dried

salt and pepper

thyme and cracked black peppercorns, to finish
rocket and pickled walnuts, to accompany

1 Place the pheasants in a small roasting tin and smear with 75 g (3 oz) of the butter.

2 Roast, breast-side down, at 200°C (400°F) mark 6 for 1 hour. Add the garlic cloves, nutmeg, peppercorns, wine, gin and thyme to the tin. Cover with foil and cook at 170°C (325°F) mark 3 for 2 hours. Cool a little.

3 Lift the pheasants out of the cooking juices. Strip away the skin and bones and coarsely shred the flesh. Season with salt and pepper, then pack tightly into a shallow, earthenware, 2.3 litre (4 pint) dish. Skim off the fat from the cooled cooking liquid; reserve the fat. Strain the juices over the pheasant, cover and chill for 1 hour.

4 Melt the remaining butter. Skim off the foam, add the reserved fat, extra thyme and cracked peppercorns. Spoon over to cover the pheasant. Return to the refrigerator to set. Serve with rocket and walnuts.

Freezing: not suitable

Twice-baked Cauliflower Cheese Soufflés

This wonderful starter can be made ahead, then cooked from frozen. For a delicious alternative, try using courgettes or broccoli instead of cauliflower. Soufflés cooked in ceramic dishes may take a few minutes longer to cook.

Preparation time: 20 minutes
Cooking time: 1¼ hours
370 cals per serving
Serves 8

75 g (3 oz) Cheddar cheese

75 g (3 oz) Emmenthal cheese

25 g (1 oz) ground almonds

50 g (2 oz) butter, plus extra for greasing

250 g (9 oz) cauliflower florets

salt and pepper

150 ml (¼ pint) milk

40 g (1½ oz) plain flour

3 large eggs, separated

284 ml (10 fl oz) carton double cream

15 ml (1 level tbsp) grainy mustard

rocket, cherry tomatoes and black pepper, to garnish

olive oil and balsamic vinegar for drizzling

1 Finely grate the cheeses. Cook the almonds under a preheated grill, turning from time to time, until lightly toasted. Grease and base-line eight 150 ml (¼ pint) dariole moulds or ramekins with greaseproof paper, then dust with toasted ground almonds.

2 Cook the cauliflower in salted, boiling water for 5-10 minutes or until tender. Drain, plunge into iced water and drain again. Place in a food processor with the milk and process for 2-3 minutes until smooth.

3 Melt the butter in a pan, add the flour and mix to a smooth paste. Blend in the cauliflower purée, stirring; bring to the boil. Cool a little; beat in cheeses and egg yolks; season well. Whisk the whites to a soft peak; fold into the cauliflower mixture.

4 Fill the prepared moulds with the cauliflower mixture and place in a roasting tin. Add enough hot water to come halfway up the sides of the moulds. Cook at 180°C (350°F) mark 4 for 20-25 minutes or until firm to the touch in the centre. Remove from the roasting tin and cool completely. Run a knife around the edge of the soufflés; carefully turn out onto a baking sheet.

5 Meanwhile pour the cream into a wide saucepan, bring to the boil and bubble until syrupy and reduced by one-third. Add the mustard and season.

6 Spoon a little cream over the soufflés; bake at 200°C (400°F) mark 6 for 15-20 minutes or until golden. Serve immediately, garnished with rocket, tomatoes and black pepper, and drizzled with olive oil and balsamic vinegar.

Freezing: suitable at the end of step 5. Wrap separately and freeze. To use, complete the recipe, cooking the soufflés from frozen for 25-30 minutes or until golden.

Glazed Quail's Eggs with Watercress

Preparation time: 1 hour, plus chilling
Cooking time: 40 minutes
510 cals per serving
Serves 8

50 g (2 oz) washed watercress

450 g (1 lb) leeks

175 g (6 oz) plain flour

150 g (5 oz) butter

salt and pepper

12 quail's eggs

200 ml (7 fl oz) double cream

90 ml (6 tbsp) thick mayonnaise

cooked baby leeks and extra quail's eggs, to garnish

1 Remove the stalks from the watercress, then roughly chop. Set aside in the refrigerator. Halve the leeks lengthways, rinse well under cold, running water, then drain and finely slice.

2 To make the pastry, place the flour in a food processor with 100 g (3½ oz) butter and a pinch of salt and process until the mixture resembles fine crumbs. Add 30 ml (2 tbsp) iced water and pulse until the crumbs come together to make a dough. Wrap in cling film and chill for 30 minutes.

3 Roll out the pastry thinly on a lightly floured work surface. Stamp out eight rounds with a 9-10 cm (3½-4 inch) fluted cutter. Place on a baking sheet, prick with a fork and chill for 30 minutes. Cook the pastry at 200°C (400°F) mark 6 for 15 minutes until golden brown. Cool.

4 Meanwhile, cook the quail's eggs in boiling water for 2 minutes. Drain and run under cold water until cool. Peel, cover and set aside.

5 Melt the remaining butter in a heavy-based saucepan. Add the leeks and cook, stirring, for 10 minutes or until soft but not coloured. Add 150 ml (5 fl oz) cream, bring to the boil and bubble for 5 minutes, stirring occasionally, until reduced and syrupy. Remove from the heat, season

well with salt and pepper and set aside to cool.

6 Place the chopped watercress in a food processor with the remaining cream and the mayonnaise. Pulse until smooth, season, pour into a bowl, cover and set aside.

7 Return the cooled pastry rounds to a baking sheet and spoon some of the leek mixture on top of each one. Place the baking sheets on the bottom of a preheated grill for 2 minutes to warm the pastry and leek mixture through.

8 Halve the quail's eggs lengthways and arrange three halves on top of the leeks, spoon some of the watercress mayonnaise on top of the quail's eggs and return to the grill for 1 minute or until bubbling and beginning to colour. Garnish with baby leeks and unshelled quail's eggs.

Freezing: not suitable

Parma Ham with Orange and Mint

Preparation time: 20 minutes, plus marinating
Cooking time: 5 minutes
250 cals per serving
Serves 4

1 orange

30 ml (2 tbsp) virgin olive oil

45 ml (3 tbsp) sweet sherry

5 ml (1 tsp) balsamic vinegar

15 ml (1 tbsp) finely chopped fresh mint

salt and pepper

75 g (3 oz) Parma ham

1 Pare the rind from the orange and place in a small bowl with the oil. Cover and set aside for 30 minutes. Slice the orange flesh.

2 Meanwhile, pour the sherry into a small saucepan, bring to the boil and bubble to reduce by half. Remove from the heat and whisk in the balsamic vinegar and the chopped mint. Season with salt and pepper; set aside to cool.

3 Arrange the orange slices on individual plates with the ham. Add the orange-flavoured oil to the sherry mixture and drizzle over. Sprinkle with pepper just before serving.

Freezing: not suitable

Glazed Quail's Eggs with Watercress

Papaya and Prawn Salad

Papaya and Prawn Salad

After the richness of the traditional Christmas fare, this light and fresh starter makes a welcome change. If the papayas are large, you'll find two enough for six people. The dressing for the prawns can be made the day before and stored in a cool place.

Preparation time: 10-15 minutes
Cooking time: none
350 cals per serving
Serves 6

2 small red chillies

30 ml (2 tbsp) white wine vinegar

45-60 ml (3-4 tbsp) freshly squeezed lime juice (about 2 limes)

150 ml (5 fl oz) olive oil

30 ml (2 tbsp) clear honey

salt and pepper

350 g (12 oz) cooked, peeled king prawns

2-3 ripe papayas

grated lime rind, to garnish

1 Finely chop the chillies, discarding the seeds. Place in a blender or food processor with the vinegar, lime juice, olive oil, honey and salt and pepper. Blend until smooth. Stir in the prawns until coated.

2 Halve, then peel the papayas. Scoop out the black seeds and discard. Thinly slice the flesh and arrange on plates.

3 Carefully spoon the prawn mixture over the papaya slices. Serve immediately, garnished with grated lime rind.

Freezing: not suitable

main dishes

Crispy Fish Spaghetti

An excellent dish for an informal meal during the Christmas break.

Preparation time: 15 minutes, plus soaking
Cooking time: 35 minutes
860 cals per serving
Serves 4

50 g (2 oz) sultanas (optional)

50 g (2 oz) anchovy fillets

450 g (1 lb) haddock, cod or salmon fillet, skinned

2 garlic cloves

125 g (4 oz) fresh breadcrumbs, preferably made from ciabatta bread

50 g (2 oz) pine nuts

5 ml (1 tsp) fennel seeds

100 ml (4 fl oz) olive oil

60 ml (4 tbsp) chopped flat-leaf parsley

100 ml (4 fl oz) white wine

1 bay leaf

6 peppercorns

salt and pepper

350 g (12 oz) dried spaghetti or spaghettini

lemon wedges and flat-leaf parsley, to garnish

1 Soak the sultanas in 45 ml (3 tbsp) warm water for 10 minutes (if using). Drain and finely chop the anchovies, reserving the oil. Cut the fish into bite-sized pieces.

2 Peel and crush the garlic. Mix the breadcrumbs, pine nuts, fennel seeds, garlic and anchovy fillets with the anchovy and olive oil in a roasting tin. Cook at 200°C (400°F) mark 6 for 15-20 minutes, turning from time to time, until crisp and brown. Add the drained sultanas (if using) and the parsley.

3 Place the fish in a shallow ovenproof dish with the white wine, 300 ml (10 fl oz) water, the bay leaf, peppercorns and salt. Cook on the shelf below the breadcrumb mixture for 15 minutes or until just cooked. Lift the fish from the liquid and set aside.

4 Strain the cooking liquid into a wide saucepan, bring it to the boil and bubble vigorously to reduce to 45-60 ml (3-4 tbsp). Meanwhile, cook the spaghetti in boiling, salted water for 10-12 minutes or until just tender. Drain and toss into the reduced liquid. Stir over a high heat for 1-2 minutes. Add the cooked fish and turn into a hot serving dish. Spoon over the hot crisp breadcrumbs and serve immediately, garnished with lemon and parsley.

Freezing: not suitable

Plaice with Tomato and Caper Dressing

Low in fat and very healthy, this is the ideal dish to serve after an over-indulgent Christmas!

Preparation time: 15 minutes
Cooking time: 10 minutes
340 cals per serving
Serves 4

8 plaice fillets, about 550 g (1¼ lb)

75 ml (5 tbsp) tapenade (black olive paste)

150 ml (5 fl oz) dry white wine

DRESSING

1 large or 2 small tomatoes

25 g (1 oz) pitted black olives

30 ml (2 tbsp) capers

rind of ½ lemon

60 ml (4 tbsp) lemon juice

salt and pepper

60 ml (4 tbsp) olive oil

fried garlic slices and fresh basil leaves, to garnish

1 Skin the plaice if necessary, then spread the tapenade over the smoother side and roll up.

2 Place the fish in a small, flameproof casserole and pour the wine around it. Bring gently to the boil, cover, reduce the heat and simmer for 8-10 minutes until just cooked. Using a slotted spoon, remove the fish and place in a warmed serving dish. Reserve the cooking liquor.

3 To make the dressing, quarter the tomatoes, discard the seeds and cut the flesh into small pieces. Finely slice the pitted black olives.

Plaice with Tomato and Caper Dressing

4 Whisk together the remaining dressing ingredients with 60 ml (4 tbsp) reserved cooking liquor. Add the tomatoes and olives and spoon over the fish. Serve garnished with fried garlic slices and basil leaves.

Freezing: not suitable

Grilled Cod with Sweet Chilli Glaze

Grilling is one of the best methods of cooking fish and this is such an easy way to perk up a simple dish. Not only is it wonderfully quick, it also produces delicious, moist fish with a crisp skin.

Preparation time: 10 minutes
Cooking time: 5 minutes
259 cals per serving
Serves 4

1 red chilli, deseeded and finely chopped

10 ml (2 tsp) dark soy sauce

grated rind and juice of 1 lime

1.25 ml (¼ level tsp) ground allspice or six allspice berries, crushed

50 g (2 oz) light soft brown sugar

4 thick cod fillets, with skin, about 175 g (6 oz) each

fried chilli and lime rind and lime wedges, to garnish

Saffron mash (see below) and shredded, blanched green beans to accompany

1 Stir the chilli, soy sauce, lime rind and juice, allspice and sugar together.
2 Grill the cod for about 1 minute on the flesh side. Turn skin-side up and grill for 1 minute. Spoon the chilli glaze over. Return to the grill for a further 2-3 minutes until the skin is crisp and golden. Garnish with fried chilli and lime rind and the lime wedges. Serve with Saffron mash (see below) and green beans.

Freezing: not suitable

SAFFRON MASH
For a delicious, creamy mash, cook 900 g (2 lb) maincrop, peeled potatoes in boiling, salted water. Meanwhile, soak a pinch of saffron strands in 30 ml (2 tbsp) boiling water. Drain and mash the potatoes with 50 g (2 oz) butter and beat in the saffron with its soaking liquid. Sprinkle with coarse salt and serve.

Fish Tagine with Couscous

A supper dish full of the aromatic, spicy flavours characteristic of North Africa.

Preparation time: 30 minutes
Cooking time: 1½ hours
569-420 cals per serving
Serves 6-8

CHILLI PASTE

3 large chillies

2 large garlic cloves, peeled

15 ml (1 level tbsp) ground coriander

30 ml (2 level tbsp) cumin seeds

large pinch saffron threads

grated rind and juice of I lemon

30 ml (2 tbsp) olive oil

TAGINE

1.1 kg (2½ lb) firm fish fillets, such as monkfish or cod, skinned and cut into large chunks

120 ml (8 tbsp) olive oil, plus extra for drizzling

900 g (2 lb) onions, roughly chopped

450 g (1 lb) aubergines, cubed

400 g can chopped plum tomatoes

500 g carton passata

200 ml (7 fl oz) fish stock

125 g (4 oz) pitted green olives

salt and pepper

30 ml (2 level tbsp) chopped fresh coriander

30 ml (2 level tbsp) chopped fresh flat-leafed parsley or coriander leaves, to garnish

COUSCOUS

350g (12 oz) couscous

60 ml (4 level tbsp) chopped fresh mint

1 To make chilli paste, place the chillies on a baking sheet and roast at 200°C (400°F) mark 6 for 10 minutes. Cool, peel and de-seed the chillies. Place in a processor with the next six ingredients. Pulse to a fine paste.
2 To make the tagine, place the fish in a bowl with 30 ml

(2 level tbsp) of the chilli paste. Toss the fish thoroughly in the paste, then cover the bowl and chill. Leave the fish to marinate while you make the tagine sauce.

3 Heat 45 ml (3 tbsp) of the olive oil in a heatproof casserole dish – the word 'tagine' refers to the clay dish in which the stew is cooked in North Africa – and cook the onions for 10 minutes until deep golden brown. Add the remaining chilli paste and cook for a further 5 minutes.

4 Heat the remaining olive oil in a separate frying pan until hot. Add the aubergines and fry over a high heat for 10 minutes until golden brown. Add to the onions, then mix in the chopped tomatoes, passata and fish stock. Bring to the boil, then simmer gently for 30 minutes.

5 Add the marinated fish to the casserole and then the green olives; spoon some of the sauce over the fish. Season, cover and cook at 200°C (400°F) mark 6 for a further 15-20 minutes. The fish should be white rather than opaque when cooked. Season to taste.

6 Place the couscous in a bowl. Pour 450 ml (¾ pint) boiling water over, cover and leave to soak according to the packet instructions. Season, fork in the mint and drizzle with olive oil. Stir the coriander and parsley into the tagine, garnish and serve immediately with the warm couscous.

Freezing: not suitable

Saffron Scallops

Preparation time: 10 minutes
Cooking time: 15 minutes
490 cals per serving
Serves 6

75 g (3 oz) shallots
1 garlic clove
900 g (2 lb) shelled scallops
50 g (2 oz) butter
200 ml (7 fl oz) Noilly Prat or white wine
300 ml (10 fl oz) double cream
pinch of saffron strands
fresh dill sprigs, to garnish

1 Peel and finely chop shallots; peel and crush garlic. Pat the scallops dry. Melt 25 g (1 oz) butter in a non-stick frying pan and quickly fry the scallops in batches for 1-2 minutes only – they should be golden on the outside and tender on the inside. Remove from the pan and set aside.

2 Melt the remaining butter, add the shallots and garlic to the pan and cook for 4-5 minutes, stirring occasionally. Stir in the Noilly Prat or wine, cream and saffron. Bubble for 4-5 minutes or until reduced and syrupy. Return the scallops to the pan and bubble for 1-2 minutes.

3 Serve immediately, garnished with dill.

Freezing: not suitable

Saffron Scallops

Chicken and
Artichoke Pie

Chicken and Artichoke Pie

This dish tastes and looks rich, but is in fact surprisingly light in calories.

Preparation time: 20 minutes
Cooking time: 45 minutes
320 cals per serving
Serves 4

3 skinless chicken breasts, about 350 g (12 oz)

150 ml (5 fl oz) dry white wine

225 g (8 oz) reduced-fat soft cheese with garlic and herbs

400 g (14 oz) can artichoke hearts in water

salt and pepper

4 sheets filo pastry, about 40 g (1½ oz)

olive oil

5 ml (1 tsp) sesame seeds

fresh thyme, to garnish

1 Bring the chicken and wine to the boil, cover and simmer for 10 minutes. Set the chicken aside. Add the cheese to the wine and mix until smooth. Bring to the boil, then simmer until thickened.

2 Cut the chicken into bite-sized pieces. Drain and quarter the artichokes; add to the sauce with the chicken. Season with salt and pepper and mix well.

3 Place the mixture in a shallow ovenproof dish. Brush the pastry lightly with oil, scrunch slightly and place on top of the chicken. Sprinkle with sesame seeds.

4 Cook at 200°C (400°F) mark 6 for 30-35 minutes or until crisp. Serve garnished with thyme.

Freezing: not suitable

VARIATION
Replace the artichoke hearts with 225 g (8 oz) brown-cap mushrooms, cooked in a little water, seasoning and lemon juice.

Turkey Meatballs with Cranberry Dressing

This is a tasty way of using up Christmas leftovers.

Preparation time: 15 minutes
Cooking time: 10 minutes
875 cals per serving
Serves 4

CRANBERRY DRESSING

15 ml (1 tbsp) sherry or balsamic vinegar

10 ml (2 tsp) caster sugar

salt and pepper

120 ml (8 tbsp) olive oil

50 g (2 oz) fresh or frozen cranberries

MEATBALLS

125 g (4 oz) celery

50 g (2 oz) walnuts, toasted

450 g (1 lb) roast turkey meat

2 garlic cloves

15 ml (1 tbsp) olive oil

10 ml (2 tsp) fennel seeds (optional)

10 ml (2 tsp) dried oregano

30 ml (2 tbsp) cranberry sauce

125 g (4 oz) fresh breadcrumbs

2 eggs

50 g (2 oz) freshly grated Parmesan cheese

oil for frying

green salad, to serve

1 To make the dressing, mix together the vinegar and sugar in a bowl. Season with salt and pepper, then whisk in the oil and stir in the cranberries. Place in a small saucepan, bring to the boil and cook for 1 minute. Set aside to cool.

2 To make the meatballs, finely chop the celery, walnuts and turkey. Peel and crush the garlic. Heat the olive oil in a medium saucepan and add the celery, garlic, fennel seeds and oregano. Cook, stirring, for 4-5 minutes, then add the cranberry sauce. Remove and allow to cool.

3 In a bowl, mix together the turkey, celery mixture, breadcrumbs, eggs, walnuts and Parmesan cheese and season with salt and pepper. Divide the mixture into 12 balls, each the size of a golf ball.

4 Heat the oil in a deep-fat fryer and cook the meatballs for 3-4 minutes or until golden brown. Drain on kitchen paper. Serve immediately on a bed of green salad drizzled with the cranberry dressing.

Freezing: suitable, meatballs only. Open-freeze at the end of step 3. Thaw at cool room temperature for about 4 hours; chill again for 10-15 minutes. Complete as in step 4.

Turkey and Mango Curry

A quick and easy way of turning leftover turkey into an exotic supper dish. Serve with fragrant Thai rice, garnished with fried onions and toasted or dried coconut slices.

Preparation time: 10 minutes
Cooking time: 15 minutes
640 cals per serving
Serves 4

175 g (6 oz) onion

1 garlic clove

125 g (4 oz) green pepper

225 g (8 oz) cooked turkey

1 fresh mango or 400 g (14 oz) can mango pieces

30 ml (2 tbsp) oil

15 ml (1 tbsp) chopped lemon grass

20 ml (4 tsp) green Thai curry paste or mild Indian curry paste

450 ml (15 fl oz) coconut milk

salt and pepper

30 ml (2 tbsp) double cream

45 ml (3 tbsp) chopped fresh coriander (optional)

1 Peel and finely chop the onion. Peel and crush the garlic. Deseed and chop the green pepper. Cut the turkey into strips. Peel the fresh mango and cut the flesh from the stone; cut the flesh into chunks. If using canned mango, drain off the liquid.

2 Heat the oil in a frying pan, add the onion, garlic, green pepper and lemon grass. Cook for 4-5 minutes, stirring. Add the curry paste and cook for 2 minutes.

3 Stir in the coconut milk and bring to the boil. Cover and simmer for 5 minutes. Add the cooked turkey and mango, season with salt and pepper and boil for 2 minutes.

4 Just before serving, add the double cream and fresh coriander, if using.

Freezing: not suitable

Garlic Poussins with Kumquats

This impressive main course contrasts a rich, creamy sauce with the tart, fruity flavour of the kumquats and cider.

Bear in mind that the casserole dish should be large enough for the poussin halves to fit in a single layer. If your casserole is not quite large enough, use a large frying pan to brown the poussins, then transfer to the casserole.

Preparation time: 20 minutes
Cooking time: 1 hour
580 cals per serving
Serves 6

3 poussins, about 700 g (1½ lb) each

salt and pepper

225 g (8 oz) kumquats

16 garlic cloves

30 ml (2 tbsp) olive oil

25 g (1 oz) unsalted butter

2 bay leaves

450 ml (15 fl oz) dry cider

200 ml (7 fl oz) apple juice

200 ml (7 fl oz) double cream

thyme sprigs, to garnish

1 Cut both sides of the backbone of the poussins with a pair of kitchen scissors and remove. Cut the poussins in half along the breast bone line. Sprinkle the skin side liberally with 10 ml (2 tsp) salt. Halve the kumquats. Cook the whole, unpeeled garlic cloves in a pan of boiling, salted water for 4 minutes. Drain, cool slightly and peel.

2 Heat the oil in a shallow, flameproof casserole, then add the butter. When the butter begins to sizzle, add the poussin halves skin-side down and cook for 4-5 minutes or until deep golden brown. Remove the poussins with a slotted spoon. Add the kumquats and garlic cloves and stir over the heat for 2-3 minutes or until golden. Return the poussins to the casserole dish, add the bay leaves and cover.

3 Cook at 200°C (400°F) mark 6 for 30-35 minutes or until the poussins are cooked through. With a slotted spoon, lift the poussins, kumquats and six of the garlic

cloves onto a baking sheet. Cover with foil and keep warm in the oven.

4 With a wooden spoon, crush the remaining garlic cloves in the casserole to a paste. Add the cider and apple juice, bring to the boil and bubble for 7-10 minutes or until syrupy. Pour in the cream, season with salt and pepper and bring back to the boil. Simmer for 1 minute. Return the poussins, whole garlic and kumquats to the casserole, cover and cook gently for 2-3 minutes.

5 Garnish the poussins with sprigs of thyme and serve.

Freezing: not suitable

Christmas Pheasant

Preparation time: 30 minutes
Cooking time: 2¼ hours
490 cals per serving
Serves 6

225 g (8 oz) shallots or small onions

225 g (8 oz) rindless streaky bacon

brace of oven-ready pheasants

salt and pepper

30 ml (2 tbsp) oil

50 g (2 oz) butter

2 garlic cloves

300 ml (10 fl oz) Madeira

600 ml (1 pint) beef stock

sprig of fresh thyme or pinch of dried

2 bay leaves

6 juniper berries

pared rind and juice of 1 orange

90 ml (6 tbsp) redcurrant jelly

225 g (8 oz) fresh cranberries

225 g (8 oz) cooked, peeled chestnuts (canned, frozen or vacuum-packed)

fresh thyme, to garnish

1 Peel the shallots and chop the bacon. Joint both pheasants into four, discarding backbone and knuckles. Season with salt and pepper.

Christmas Pheasant

2 Heat the oil and butter in a large, flameproof casserole and brown the shallots and bacon. Remove and set aside. Add the pheasant, half at a time, and fry for 5-6 minutes or until golden. Remove the pheasant from the casserole.

3 Peel and crush the garlic and add to the casserole with half the Madeira, the stock, thyme, bay leaves, juniper berries and pared orange rind. Bring to the boil, add the pheasant. Cover and cook at 170°C (325°F) mark 3 for 1 hour.

4 Add the shallots, bacon and redcurrant jelly. Re-cover and return to the oven for 45 minutes or until the pheasant is quite tender.

5 Meanwhile, marinate the cranberries and chestnuts in the remaining Madeira and the orange juice for 30 minutes.

6 Remove the pheasant, vegetables and bacon from the liquid, cover and keep warm. Bubble the sauce for about 5 minutes to reduce to a syrupy consistency. Add the cranberry and chestnut mixture and simmer for a further 5 minutes. Adjust the seasoning and spoon this sauce over the pheasant. Serve garnished with fresh thyme.

Freezing: suitable at the end of step 4. Thaw overnight at cool room temperature. Bring to the boil, cover and cook at 180°C (350°F) mark 4 for about 40 minutes. Complete as above.

Pan-fried Guinea Fowl with Red Wine Sauce

This elegant dish is simple to prepare, making it a good choice for fast entertaining.

A celeriac and potato purée would make the ideal seasonal accompaniment – simply cook 700 g (1½ lb) each peeled and diced celeriac and potatoes in boiling salted water with 15 ml (1 tbsp) vinegar and 3 garlic cloves for 20-25 minutes. Mash, then beat in butter and cream to taste; add chopped chives and season well.

Preparation time: 5 minutes
Cooking time: 25-30 minutes
435 cals per serving
Serves 6

175 g (6 oz) rindless streaky bacon

25 g (1 oz) butter

15 ml (1 tbsp) oil

6 guinea fowl or chicken breast fillets, about 150 g (5 oz) each

225 g (8 oz) button mushrooms

225 g (8 oz) frozen button onions

90 ml (6 tbsp) brandy

350 ml (12 fl oz) red wine

750 ml (1¼ pints) chicken stock

60 ml (4 tbsp) redcurrant jelly

salt and pepper

1 Chop the bacon. Melt the butter and oil in a frying pan, add the guinea fowl and cook, skin-side down, over a high heat for 3 minutes on each side or until golden. Transfer to an ovenproof dish and place in the oven, at 150°C (300°F) mark 2, to finish cooking while you make the sauce.

2 Add the bacon, mushrooms and onions to the frying pan. Cook for 4-5 minutes or until golden. Remove with a slotted spoon and set aside. Add the brandy, wine, stock and jelly to the frying pan. Bring to the boil and bubble furiously for 15-20 minutes or until the sauce is syrupy.

3 Return the guinea fowl, bacon, mushrooms and onions to the pan. Bring to the boil and season with salt and pepper. Serve at once.

Freezing: not suitable

Duck with Cardamom Sauce

Ginger wine, a traditional drink at Christmas, is used in this sauce to complement the spiciness of the green cardamom pods.

For a quick and colourful warm salad to serve with the duck, cut about 175 g (6 oz) mixed vegetables such as carrots, peppers, courgettes and spring onions into fine, matchstick-length strips. Stir-fry with 350 g (12 oz) fresh spinach and one red chilli in 15 ml (1 tbsp) oil with a dash of sesame oil and a squeeze of fresh lime juice, if wished. Season and serve immediately, sprinkled with 25 g (1 oz) very finely chopped, roasted peanuts.

Preparation time: 15 minutes
Cooking time: 2½ hours
400 cals per serving
Serves 6

6 duck legs, about 2 kg (4½ lb)

350 g (12 oz) onions

5 cm (2 inch) piece fresh root ginger

125 g (4 oz) butter

15 ml (1 tbsp) caster sugar

8 whole green cardamom pods

1.7 litres (3 pints) chicken stock

300 ml (10 fl oz) ginger wine

150 ml (5 fl oz) dry white wine

salt and pepper

45 ml (3 tbsp) orange juice

15 ml (1 tbsp) lemon juice

5 ml (1 tsp) oil

10 ml (2 tsp) coarse sea salt

chopped fresh coriander, to garnish

1 Place the duck legs in a large saucepan and cover with cold water. Bring to the boil, cover and simmer gently on a low heat for 2 hours.

2 Meanwhile, make the cardamom sauce. Peel and finely chop the onions; peel and grate the ginger. Gently fry the onions in 50 g (2 oz) of the butter for 10 minutes or until softened. Add the sugar, ginger and the seeds from one cardamom pod and continue to cook, stirring, until the onion has turned a very dark golden brown.

Duck with Cardamom Sauce

3 Add the stock and bring to the boil. Bubble, uncovered, for about 30 minutes or until reduced by half. Add the ginger wine and white wine and bubble again for about 30 minutes or until reduced by half again and the sauce is a thin syrup consistency. Season with salt and pepper and stir in the orange and lemon juice to taste.

4 Return the sauce to the boil and whisk in 25 g (1 oz) of the remaining butter. Strain the onions from the sauce and place in a small saucepan with the remaining 25 g (1 oz) butter. Set aside the onions and sauce.

5 Drain and dry the cooked duck on kitchen paper and place on a rack over a roasting tin. Rub with the oil and sprinkle liberally with the salt. Split the remaining cardamom pods and sprinkle over the duck.

6 Roast at 230°C (450°F) mark 8 for 20-25 minutes or until the duck skin is very crisp. Gently reheat the onions with the butter, bring the cardamom sauce to the boil, and serve with the duck. Garnish with coriander and serve at once.

Freezing: suitable. Cook the duck as step 1. Make the sauce to the end of step 3, then freeze separately. Thaw overnight at cool room temperature. Complete from step 4.

Beef Medallions with Stilton Mousse

This elegant dinner party dish is surprisingly quick to make.

Preparation time: 15 minutes
Cooking time: 15 minutes
630 cals per serving
Serves 6

225 g (8 oz) skinless chicken breast fillets, chilled

300 ml (10 fl oz) double cream, chilled

225 g (8 oz) crumbled Stilton cheese

salt and pepper

275 g (10 oz) celery

25 g (1 oz) butter

six 150 g (5 oz) fillet steaks

15 ml (1 tbsp) chopped fresh parsley

squeeze of lemon juice

extra Stilton, to crumble (optional)

1 Blend the chicken in a food processor until smooth. Add the cream and pulse for 2-3 seconds or until the cream is just combined. Add the Stilton cheese to the chicken in the same way. Season with salt and pepper and refrigerate for 10 minutes.

2 Meanwhile, slice the celery into matchsticks. Melt the butter in a medium saucepan, add the celery and cook gently, covered, for about 5 minutes or until just tender. Keep warm.

3 Heat a non-stick frying pan and fry the steaks on both sides for about 3 minutes for rare (5 minutes for medium; 6-7 minutes for well done). Be careful to time your steaks accurately. Place on a hot baking sheet.

4 Divide the chilled Stilton mixture among the medallions and spread evenly over the top of each one. Grill for about 6 minutes or until the mousse turns golden brown and is firm and cooked through.

5 Add the chopped parsley and lemon juice to the celery and serve alongside the beef medallions. Crumble a little extra Stilton over the steaks, if wished.

Freezing: not suitable

Lamb with Chestnut and Cherry Tomato Relish

If you do not have the time to cook and peel fresh chestnuts, you can always use canned, frozen or vacuum-packed chestnuts for this dish.

Preparation time: 10-15 minutes
Cooking time: 20 minutes
450 cals per serving
Serves 6

175 g (6 oz) cooked, peeled chestnuts

75 g (3 oz) cherry tomatoes

175 g (6 oz) rindless streaky bacon

3 racks of lamb, trimmed, about 900 g (2 lb) total weight

3 garlic cloves

pepper

100 ml (4 fl oz) olive oil

60 ml (4 tbsp) finely chopped fresh parsley

10 ml (2 tsp) caster sugar

30 ml (2 tbsp) balsamic vinegar

flat-leaf parsley, to garnish

1 Roughly chop the chestnuts and halve the tomatoes. Snip the bacon with scissors. Rub the lamb with 1 garlic clove and pepper.

2 Place the lamb racks in a shallow roasting tin and scatter the bacon on top. Cook at 240°C (475°F) mark 9 for 15-20 minutes for medium (25-30 minutes for well done).

3 Meanwhile, peel and crush the remaining garlic and whisk into the olive oil, with the parsley, sugar and balsamic vinegar. Add the chestnuts and cherry tomatoes.

4 Remove the lamb from the oven and leave to rest in a warm place for 5 minutes. Stir the pan juices into the chestnut relish.

5 Halve each rack and arrange on warm plates with the relish. Garnish with parsley and serve.

Freezing: not suitable

Lamb with Chestnut and Cherry Tomato Relish

Grilled Lamb with Garlic and Lemon

Try this speedy way with lamb for an instant meal with friends.

Preparation time: 5 minutes
Cooking time: 15 minutes
525 cals per serving
Serves 6

900 g-1.1 kg (2-2½ lb) boneless leg steaks of lamb
3 garlic cloves

grated rind and juice of 1 lemon
150 ml (5 fl oz) olive oil
salt and pepper
flat-leaf parsley and sliced lemon, to garnish

1 Place the lamb in a foil-lined grill pan. Peel and slice the garlic, then add to the lamb with the lemon rind and juice and olive oil. Season with pepper.

2 Grill for about 7-10 minutes on each side, until well-charred and just cooked through. Season with salt and serve, garnished with flat-leaf parsley and sliced lemon.

Freezing: not suitable

Mexican Hotpot

Preparation time: 5 minutes
Cooking time: 1 hour
520 cals per serving
Serves 6

30 ml (2 tbsp) oil

1 large onion, roughly chopped

2 garlic cloves, finely chopped

15 ml (1 level tbsp) mild chilli powder

450 g (1 lb) minced beef or lamb

30 ml (2 level tbsp) tomato paste

400 g can plum tomatoes, chopped

420 g can red kidney beans in chilli sauce

440 g can mixed beans in spicy sauce

450 ml (¾ pint) beef or lamb stock

salt and pepper

125 g (4 oz) tortilla chips

75 g (3 oz) grated hard cheese

Jalapeno chillies and flat-leafed parsley, to garnish (optional)

crisp green salad, to accompany

1 Heat the oil in a large frying pan, add the onion and cook for 10 minutes or until soft and brown. Add the garlic and chilli powder and cook for 1 minute. Add the minced beef and cook, stirring from time to time, for 15-20 minutes or until the mince has broken up into small pieces. Stir in the tomato paste and cook for 2 minutes. Add the canned tomatoes, the beans and stock and season well. Bring to the boil and simmer for 30-35 minutes or until thick and rich.

2 Transfer to a 1.7 litre (3 pint) capacity ovenproof dish. Sprinkle the tortilla chips and the cheese on top. Place under the grill for 1-2 minutes or until golden. Garnish with the sliced chillies and parsley and serve with salad.

Freezing: not suitable

Roast Pork with Apple and Saffron Chutney

Preparation time: 20 minutes, plus cooling
Cooking time: 1½ hours, plus 20 minutes resting
530 cals per serving
Serves 8

30 g (1¼ oz) butter

75 g (3 oz) caster sugar

2 large Cox's orange pippin apples, 350 g (12 oz), peeled, cored and roughly diced

75 ml (5 tbsp) cider vinegar

pinch of saffron threads

100 g (3½ oz) dried cranberries

50 g (2 oz) sultanas

350 g (12 oz) pumpkin, peeled and diced

½ red chilli, de-seeded and finely chopped

2.3 kg (5 lb) loin pork, boned, skin finely scored (choose a thin, narrow joint)

salt

chopped flat-leafed parsley and saffron threads, to garnish

1 Melt the butter and sugar in a heavy-based saucepan until golden. Add the next seven ingredients and cook, stirring, over a medium heat until caramelised. Add 30 ml (2 tbsp) water and simmer for 5-8 minutes. Set chutney aside to cool.

2 Slit pork lengthways, almost through the muscle, and open out. Place two-thirds of the chutney down the middle and roll up. Tie the joint at intervals with string, but not too tightly. Reserve the leftover chutney.

3 Sprinkle pork skin generously with salt, then cook at 200°C (400°F) mark 6 for 1¼ hours. Add the reserved chutney to the roasting tin for last 10 minutes of cooking time, then remove pork from oven, cover loosely and rest for 20 minutes. Slice the pork thickly and garnish with parsley and saffron threads.

Freezing: not suitable

Glazed Pork Loin with Fig Stuffing

Glazed Pork Loin with Fig Stuffing

It is important to score the crackling deeply to ensure a crisp result. Accompany the roast with a gravy made from the pan juices if wished, and seasonal vegetables.

Preparation time: 30 minutes
Cooking time: 2 hours
480 cals per serving
Serves 6

1.4 kg (3 lb) boned loin of pork, skin well scored

salt and pepper

60 ml (4 tbsp) clear honey

10 ml (2 tsp) mustard powder

finely grated rind of 1 lemon

rosemary sprigs and a few fresh figs, to garnish

FIG STUFFING

4 shallots

1 garlic clove

225 g (8 oz) no-soak dried figs

1 eating apple

2 fresh rosemary sprigs

50 g (2 oz) butter

finely grated rind and juice of 1 lemon

45 ml (3 tbsp) dry sherry

1 For the stuffing, peel and finely chop the shallots. Peel and crush the garlic. Roughly chop the figs. Peel, core and finely chop the apple. Chop the rosemary.

2 Melt the butter in a saucepan and add the shallots and garlic. Cook for 5-10 minutes until soft and golden. Stir in the figs, apple, rosemary, lemon rind and juice, and sherry. Cook, stirring, for 5 minutes until slightly softened and most of the liquid has evaporated. Cool.

3 Lay the pork loin, skin-side down, on a clean surface. Season well with salt and pepper and spread the stuffing along the middle. Roll up and tie at intervals with fine string. Place in a roasting tin and roast at 190°C (375°F) mark 5 for 1 hour.

4 Meanwhile, place the honey, mustard and lemon rind in a saucepan and heat gently, stirring. Brush over the pork skin and roast for a further 45 minutes, basting every 15 minutes.

5 Leave to rest in a warm place for 15 minutes. Carve into thick slices and serve garnished with sprigs of rosemary and a few fresh figs.

Freezing: not suitable

VARIATION

Replace the figs with no-soak prunes or apricots. Use thyme instead of rosemary.

Sticky Glazed Ham with Spiced Oranges

Forward planning is required for this dish as the spiced oranges need to be prepared two weeks in advance.

Preparation time: 30 minutes, plus soaking and storing
Cooking time: 2¼ hours
270 cals per serving
Serves 6

1.1 kg (2½ lb) gammon joint

125 g (4 oz) each carrot, onion, celery

15 ml (1 tbsp) Dijon mustard

15 ml (1 tbsp) soft light brown (muscovado) sugar

45 ml (3 tbsp) marmalade

300 ml (10 fl oz) cider

SPICED ORANGES

1.1 kg (2½ lb) oranges

750 ml (1¼ pint) white wine vinegar

1.1 kg (2½ lb) granulated sugar

half cinnamon stick

30 cloves

1 To make the spiced oranges, slice the whole oranges thinly and place in a large pan with just enough water to cover. Bring to the boil and simmer for 5 minutes, then drain and set aside.

2 Add the vinegar, granulated sugar, cinnamon and cloves and bring to the boil, stirring occasionally. Return the orange slices and simmer for 30 minutes.

3 Lift the orange slices out of the syrup and place in sterilised vinegar-proof jars. Boil the syrup hard until reduced to 1.1 litres (2 pints). Pour over the oranges, cover and leave in a cool, dark place for at least two weeks.

4 The day before serving, cover the gammon in cold water and leave to soak overnight.

5 Peel and roughly chop the vegetables. Drain the gammon and place in a large saucepan with the chopped vegetables. Add enough water to cover. Bring slowly to the boil, then cover and simmer very gently for 1 hour. Leave to cool in the water for 1 hour. Drain and remove the rind.

6 Place the gammon in a small roasting tin. Combine the mustard with the sugar and marmalade and spread over the ham fat. Pour in the cider; cook at 200°C (400°F) mark 6 for 20-30 minutes until the fat is crisp and golden, basting occasionally. Cool.

7 Serve the ham thinly sliced with the spiced oranges.

Freezing: Suitable, cooked ham only; freeze at the end of step 6. Thaw overnight in the refrigerator and serve cold.

Venison and Cranberry Daube

Preparation time: 1 hour, plus marinating
Cooking time: about 2½ hours
490 cals per serving
Serves 6

1 kg (2¼ lb) stewing venison

MARINADE

125 g (4 oz) each onion, carrot and celery

5 ml (1 tsp) black peppercorns

4 garlic cloves

finely grated rind and juice of 2 oranges

15 ml (1 tbsp) dried thyme

75 ml (3 fl oz) olive oil

DAUBE

450 g (1 lb) shallots or button onions

30 ml (2 tbsp) oil

75 g (3 oz) butter

45 ml (3 tbsp) plain flour

100 ml (4 fl oz) red wine vinegar

30 ml (2 tbsp) redcurrant jelly

300 ml (10 fl oz) port

300 ml (10 fl oz) beef stock

salt and pepper

1 fresh bay leaf, plus extra to garnish

125 g (4 oz) dried cranberries

Venison and Cranberry Daube

1 Cut the venison into 4 cm (1½ inch) cubes. For the marinade, peel and roughly dice the onion and carrot; trim and dice the celery. Roughly crush the peppercorns. Peel and crush the garlic. Place the venison in a bowl with the vegetables, orange rind, peppercorns, garlic, thyme and olive oil. Cover; refrigerate overnight.

2 For the daube, trim the root end of the shallots, then pour over boiling water to cover and leave for 5-10 minutes. Drain and remove the skins. Heat the oil in a large flameproof casserole and add 25 g (1 oz) butter.

3 Drain the venison and vegetables, reserving the marinade. Brown the venison in small batches over a brisk heat, adding 25 g (1 oz) more butter to the casserole when necessary. Remove the venison and set aside. Lower the heat, add the diced vegetables and fry for 2-3 minutes. Remove and set aside with the venison. Add the remaining 25 g (1 oz) butter and fry the shallots for 4-5

minutes or until golden. Remove and set aside.

4 Add the flour and cook, stirring, for 1-2 minutes. Add the vinegar, redcurrant jelly, port, stock and reserved marinade. Bring to the boil and bubble for 1-2 minutes.

5 Return the venison and diced vegetables to the pan. Season with salt and pepper and add one bay leaf. Bring to simmering point, cover tightly and cook at 180°C (350°F) mark 4 for 30 minutes.

6 Reduce the oven to 150°C (300°F) mark 2. Add the reserved shallots, orange juice and cranberries and cook for 1¾ hours or until very tender.

7 Remove the casserole from the oven and adjust the seasoning. Garnish with fresh bay leaves and serve.

Freezing: suitable at the end of step 6. Thaw overnight at cool room temperature. Bring the casserole to the boil, then cover and reheat at 180°C (350°F) mark 4 for 30-40 minutes.

Roasted Vegetable Moussaka

Preparation time: 20 minutes
Cooking time: 1 hour 55 minutes
545 cals per serving
Serves 10

700 g (1½ lb) potatoes, preferably sweet potatoes

salt and pepper

450 g (1 lb) tomatoes, preferably plum

700 g (1½ lb) aubergines

225 g (8 oz) courgettes

225 g (8 oz) fennel

450 g (1 lb) red peppers

450 g (1 lb) red onions

4 garlic cloves

150 ml (5 fl oz) olive oil

15 ml (3 tsp) dried thyme

150 ml (5 fl oz) white wine

45 ml (3 tbsp) sun-dried tomato paste

10 ml (2 tsp) sugar

450 g (1 lb) passata

350 g (12 oz) goats' cheese

50 g (2 oz) freshly grated Parmesan cheese

1 Peel and slice the potatoes into 5 mm (½ inch) slices. Boil in salted water for 4 minutes, drain. Cut the tomatoes into 5 mm (¼ inch) slices.

2 Cut the aubergines and courgettes in 1 cm (½ inch) slices. Cut the fennel into large pieces. Deseed the peppers and cut into large chunks. Peel the onions and cut into large chunks. Place the aubergines, fennel, peppers, potatoes, onions and the unpeeled garlic cloves with the oil into 2 large roasting tins. Season well with salt and pepper and sprinkle over 10 ml (2 tsp) thyme.

3 Cook uncovered at 230°C (450°F) mark 8 for 45 minutes, stirring occasionally. For the final 10 minutes add the tomatoes and courgettes.

4 Lift out the garlic cloves, remove the skins and lightly mash with a fork. Place in a saucepan with the wine, sun-dried tomato paste and sugar. Bring to the boil and bubble for 2 minutes. Add the passata and bubble for a further 8

minutes. Season with salt and pepper.

5 Layer half the roasted vegetables in a large ovenproof dish with half the tomato sauce. Layer the remaining vegetables and sauce.

6 Cover and cook at 200°C (400°F) mark 6 for 45 minutes. Cut the goats' cheese into 1 cm (½ inch) thick slices. Uncover and place the cheese on top, sprinkle over the Parmesan and remaining thyme and cook for 15 minutes. If the cheese does not brown sufficiently, slip the dish under a preheated grill for 3 minutes.

Freezing: not suitable

Vegetable Ragout with Cheese Polenta Topping

A rich, thick stew of leeks, tomatoes, aubergines and chick peas, topped with a golden crust of cheesy, herby polenta, this dish will appeal to meat eaters and vegetarians alike.

Preparation time: 40 minutes, plus cooling
Cooking time: 30 minutes
750-560 cals per serving
Serves 6-8

700 g (1½ lb) aubergines

salt and pepper

450 g (1 lb) leeks

2 garlic cloves

450 g (1 lb) ripe red tomatoes

150 ml (5 fl oz) olive oil

150 ml (5 fl oz) dry white wine

400 g (14 oz) can chopped tomatoes

30 ml (2 tbsp) sun-dried tomato paste

400 g (14 oz) can chick peas

POLENTA TOPPING

375 g (13 oz) packet quick-cook polenta

125 g (4 oz) Gruyère cheese, grated

90 ml (6 tbsp) freshly grated Parmesan cheese

15 ml (1 tbsp) dried mixed Provençal herbs (or fresh herbs if available)

Vegetable Ragout with Cheese Polenta Topping

1 Cut the aubergines into large chunks, place in a colander and sprinkle with salt. Leave to drain for 30 minutes.

2 Slice the leeks. Peel and crush the garlic. Plunge the tomatoes into boiling water for 30 seconds. Refresh under cold water and slip off the skins. Halve, deseed, then cut into quarters.

3 Heat 30 ml (2 tbsp) olive oil in a large saucepan and add the leeks and garlic. Fry for 5 minutes until softened and beginning to brown, but not disintegrate.

4 Add the fresh tomatoes and wine and cook over a high heat for about 7 minutes until the tomatoes have softened and the wine has evaporated. Stir in the canned tomatoes, tomato paste and drained chick peas.

5 Rinse the aubergines thoroughly, then pat dry with kitchen paper. Heat the remaining olive oil in a frying pan and fry the aubergines over a high heat until browning. Stir into the leek and tomato mixture. Pour into a large shallow ovenproof dish and set aside until cold.

6 Bring 1.6 litres (2¾ pints) water to the boil in a large heavy-based saucepan, with 10 ml (2 tsp) salt added. Sprinkle in the polenta, stirring all the time. Cook, stirring for 5-10 minutes until thick. Stir in the Gruyère, 60 ml (4 tbsp) Parmesan cheese, plenty of salt and pepper and the herbs. Spread in a shallow tin to a thickness of 2 cm (¾ inch) and allow to cool. When cold, stamp into rounds with a 4 cm (1½ inch) plain cutter.

7 Arrange the polenta in overlapping circles around the dish, leaving a space in the middle.

8 Sprinkle with the remaining Parmesan cheese and bake at 200°C (400°F) mark 6 for about 30 minutes until golden brown and heated through. Serve immediately.

Freezing: suitable at the end of step 7. Thaw overnight at cool room temperature and complete step 8.

Spinach and Mushroom Pancakes

Any left-over pancakes can be frozen and used later for another dish.

If you want to cut down on preparation time, use ready-made pancakes which are available from supermarkets.

Preparation time: 1 hour, plus standing and soaking
Cooking time: 1½ hours
375 cals per serving
Serves 4

50 g (2 oz) plain white flour

50 g (2 oz) plain wholemeal flour

1 egg

350 ml (12 fl oz) skimmed milk

salt and pepper

300 ml (10 fl oz) vegetable stock

25 g (1 oz) dried mushrooms

15 ml (1 tbsp) vegetable oil, plus extra for greasing

450 g (1 lb) fresh spinach, washed and prepared, or 350 g (12 oz) frozen leaf spinach, thawed

225 g (8 oz) reduced-fat soft cheese

450 g (1 lb) brown-cap mushrooms

1 bunch spring onions

flat-leaf parsley, to garnish

1 Blend together the flours, egg, milk and a pinch of salt in a food processor. Cover and set aside for 30 minutes. Pour the stock over the dried mushrooms and leave to soak for 30 minutes.

2 Lightly oil a small non-stick crêpe pan. When hot, add enough batter to coat the base of the pan thinly. Cook the pancake for 1-2 minutes until golden brown, then turn and cook for a further 30 seconds. Transfer to a plate. Continue with the remaining batter to make 10-12 pancakes.

3 Cook the spinach in a pan for 2-3 minutes until just wilted. Cool, squeeze out the liquid and chop. Mix with the soft cheese and season with salt and pepper to taste.

4 Roughly chop the brown-cap mushrooms and spring onions. Heat 15 ml (1 tbsp) oil in a pan, add the chopped mushrooms and spring onions and cook for about 10 minutes or until lightly browned. Add the soaked dried mushrooms and stock, bring to the boil, then reduce heat and simmer for 15-20 minutes or until syrupy. Season. Blend half the mushroom mixture in a food processor until smooth. Return to the pan and combine with the remaining mushrooms.

5 Place half the spinach mixture in a lightly oiled, 1.1 litre (2 pint) shallow, ovenproof dish. Using about six pancakes, layer them with the mushroom mixture and remaining spinach mixture, finishing with a mushroom layer.

6 Cook at 200°C (400°F) mark 6 for 30 minutes or until well browned and hot. Serve garnished with flat-leaf parsley.

Freezing: suitable, pancakes only. Interleave with greaseproof paper, wrap and freeze. Thaw overnight at cool room temperature and reheat in the oven.

Spinach and Mushroom Pancakes

accompaniments

Brussels Sprouts with Chestnuts and Onions

If oven space is tight, fry the onions and lemon rind in butter until golden. Add the chestnuts and parboiled sprouts; stir for 3-4 minutes or until piping hot.

Preparation time: 20 minutes
Cooking time: 45 minutes
225 cals per serving
Serves 8

900 g (2 lb) Brussels sprouts

salt and pepper

450 g (1 lb) small onions, preferably red

125 g (4 oz) butter

grated rind of 1 lemon

450 g (1 lb) cooked, peeled, vacuum-packed chestnuts

1 Trim the sprouts, then cook in boiling, salted water for 3-4 minutes only. Drain well. Peel and quarter the onions.
2 Melt half the butter in a roasting tin. Add the onions with the lemon rind, then roast at 190°C (375°F) mark 5 for 35 minutes or until golden.
3 Stir in the chestnuts, sprouts and remaining butter, and season with salt and pepper. Return to the oven for a further 5 minutes or until piping hot.

Freezing: not suitable

Brussels Sprouts with Chestnuts and Onions

Creamy Brussels Sprouts

Preparation time: 15 minutes
Cooking time: 25 minutes, plus 30 minutes infusing
170-135 cals per serving
Serves 8-10

600 ml (1 pint) milk

1 thick slice each onion and celery

6 peppercorns

1 small bay leaf

1.1 kg (2½ lb) Brussels sprouts, lightly trimmed

salt and pepper

40 g (1½ oz) butter

40 g (1½ oz) plain flour

½ whole nutmeg, grated – about 5 ml (1 level tsp)

60 ml (4 tbsp) single cream

oregano sprigs, flat-leafed parsley and grated nutmeg, to garnish

1 Place the milk in a saucepan with the onion, celery, peppercorns and bay leaf. Bring to the boil, remove from the heat and leave to infuse for 20-30 minutes.

2 Meanwhile, cook the sprouts in a pan of boiling salted water until just tender. Drain and plunge into a bowl of icy water. Drain again and dry well.

3 Strain and reserve milk. Melt butter in a heavy-based saucepan. Off the heat, add flour and stir until smooth. Stir in the milk and mix until smooth. Return to the heat and bring to the boil, stirring. Simmer for 1-2 minutes, add nutmeg and season. Float cream on top.

4 In a food processor, pulse sprouts briefly until roughly chopped. Combine with sauce. Place in a pan over a low heat and stir until hot. Garnish to serve.

Freezing: suitable at the end of step 4 but don't reheat. Pack and freeze. Thaw overnight at cool room temperature, then reheat as above.

Roasted Root Vegetables

You can easily adapt this recipe by substituting other vegetables, or by adding flavourings such as herbs or cloves of garlic.

Preparation time: 30 minutes
Cooking time: 1 hour 10 minutes
250 cals per serving
Serves 8

1.8 kg (4 lb) parsnips and old potatoes

150 ml (¼ pint) oil

coarse sea salt

125 g (4 oz) finely grated Parmesan cheese, to garnish

1 Peel the parsnips and cut them into large, even-sized chunks. Peel the potatoes if wished, and cut them into wedges. Par-boil the parsnips and potatoes for about 5-10 minutes to soften them.

2 Drain thoroughly, then roughen the potato edges using a fork, or toss them in the pan or a colander.

3 Heat the oil in a roasting tin on the hob. Spoon in the potatoes, baste with the oil and sprinkle with coarse sea salt. Roast on the top shelf of the oven at 190°C (375°F) mark 5 for 15 minutes, then add parsnips to the tin and continue roasting for about 45 minutes, basting the vegetables occasionally.

4 Serve sprinkled with coarse salt and finely grated Parmesan cheese.

Freezing: not suitable

Mashed Potatoes with Onions and Melting Cheese

Mashed Potatoes with Onions and Melting Cheese

Preparation time: 10 minutes
Cooking time: 20 minutes
560 cals per serving
Serves 4

900 g (2 lb) potatoes

salt and pepper

350 g (12 oz) onions

45 ml (3 tbsp) olive oil

75 g (3 oz) butter

90 ml (6 tbsp) single cream or milk

75 g (3 oz) coarsely grated Cheddar cheese

1 Peel and roughly chop the potatoes. Cook in boiling, salted water until tender.

2 Meanwhile, peel and thinly slice the onions and fry in the olive oil, stirring over a medium to high heat, until golden and some of the onions are crisp.

3 Drain and mash the potatoes with the butter and single cream or milk. Season to taste with salt and pepper.

4 Stir the coarsely grated cheese into the hot onions and spoon over the mashed potatoes. Serve immediately.

Freezing: not suitable

Celeriac with Apples and Crème Fraîche

Preparation time: 15 minutes
Cooking time: 40 minutes
115 cals per serving
Serves 4

1.1 kg (2½ lb) celeriac
salt and pepper
5 ml (1 tsp) lemon juice
450 g (1 lb) eating apples
30 ml (2 tbsp) reduced-fat crème fraîche
crème fraîche and chopped chives, to garnish

1 Peel the celeriac and cut into chunks. Place in a saucepan of cold, salted water with the lemon juice. Bring to the boil, cover and simmer for 25-30 minutes.

2 Peel, core and slice the apples; add to the celeriac. Simmer for 5 minutes. Drain well and mash in the pan over a low heat.

3 Beat in the crème fraîche, season with salt and pepper and serve garnished with crème fraîche and chives.

Freezing: not suitable

Honey-glazed Shallots

An excellent accompaniment to roast poultry, these shallots can be completed and refrigerated up to one day ahead, then reheated over a low heat.

Preparation time: 15 minutes
Cooking time: 25 minutes
95 cals per serving
Serves 4

450 g (1 lb) shallots
25 g (1 oz) butter
15 ml (1 tbsp) clear honey
juice of ½ lemon
15 ml (1 tbsp) Worcestershire sauce
15 ml (1 tbsp) balsamic vinegar
salt and pepper

1 Peel the shallots and place in a saucepan with just enough cold water to cover. Bring to the boil, then simmer for 5 minutes. Drain well.

2 Add the butter to the pan with all the remaining ingredients.

3 Stir until the shallots are coated with the glaze. Cover and cook over a low heat, stirring occasionally, for about 20 minutes or until the shallots are tender. Remove the lid and continue to cook for a further 2-3 minutes until any remaining liquid is thick and syrupy.

Freezing: not suitable

Honey-glazed Shallots

Yellow Split Peas with Coconut

Preparation time: 5 minutes
Cooking time: about 30 minutes
200 cals per serving
Serves 6

275 g (10 oz) yellow split peas
salt and pepper
75 g (3 oz) creamed coconut
60 ml (4 tbsp) single cream (optional)
chopped fresh coriander, to garnish

1 Cook the split peas in boiling, salted water for 30-35 minutes or until just tender. Grate the coconut.

2 Drain the peas, return to the pan and stir in the coconut until melted throughout. Add the cream, if using; adjust the seasoning. Serve garnished with coriander.

Freezing: not suitable

Beetroot, Cucumber and Spring Onion Salad

You can buy ready-cooked beetroot for convenience, but cooking your own is well worth the effort. Cooked beetroot keeps well in the refrigerator and is a good base for salads and hot dishes. Pickled beetroot is not suitable, because it would mask the delicate flavours of the salad.

Preparation time: 25 minutes
Cooking time: none
360 cals per serving
Serves 6

700 g (1½ lb) cooked beetroot
1 medium cucumber
4 pickled dill cucumbers
6 spring onions

DRESSING
150 ml (5 fl oz) sunflower oil
1 egg
45 ml (3 tbsp) Dijon mustard
30 ml (2 tbsp) chopped fresh dill
5 ml (1 tsp) raspberry or red wine vinegar
squeeze of lemon juice
salt and pepper
200 ml (7 fl oz) soured cream or crème fraîche
dill sprigs, to garnish

1 Peel the beetroot and cut into sticks. Halve the cucumber and cut into sticks – the same size as the beetroot. Dice the dill cucumbers. Trim and slice the spring onions.

2 Arrange the beetroot on a flat plate, or in a shallow dish. Arrange the cucumber over the beetroot. Scatter the diced dill cucumber and spring onions on top.

3 To make the dressing, place 45 ml (3 tbsp) sunflower oil in a blender or food processor and add the egg, mustard, dill, wine vinegar, lemon juice, and salt and pepper. Blend for a few seconds until evenly mixed and thickened. With the machine running, pour in the rest of the oil in a thin steady stream. Stir in the soured cream or crème fraîche.

4 Drizzle the dressing over the salad and garnish with dill sprigs to serve.

Freezing: not suitable

Beetroot, Cucumber and Spring Onion Salad

Spinach and Carrot Salad

Preparation time: 15 minutes
Cooking time: 3 minutes
140 cals per serving
Serves 12

350 g (12 oz) carrots

225 g (8 oz) French beans

salt and pepper

350 g (12 oz) spinach

1 garlic clove

10 ml (2 tsp) soy and 5-spice sauce

10 ml (2 tsp) clear honey

15 ml (1 tbsp) cider vinegar

60 ml (4 tbsp) olive oil

1 Peel and slice the carrots; top and tail the French beans. Cook the carrots in boiling, salted water for 2 minutes; the French beans for 1 minute. Rinse in cold water. Wash, dry and tear the spinach. Peel and crush the garlic.

2 Whisk together the remaining ingredients to make the dressing. Season with salt and pepper.

3 Toss the vegetables and dressing together and serve.

Freezing: not suitable

Winter Squash Salad

Preparation time: 15 minutes
Cooking time: 55 minutes
275-185 cals per serving
Serves 4-6

125 g (4 oz) onions

225 g (8 oz) yellow butternut squash

2 garlic cloves

225 g (8 oz) courgettes

225 g (8 oz) plum tomatoes

50 g (2 oz) feta cheese

75 ml (5 tbsp) olive oil

30 ml (2 tbsp) chopped fresh herbs, such as chives,

mint or flat-leaf parsley

salt and pepper

50 g (2 oz) chopped black and green olives

1 Peel and finely slice the onions and squash. Peel and crush the garlic. Finely slice the courgettes and tomatoes. Crumble the cheese.

2 Heat 30 ml (2 tbsp) oil in a saucepan and fry the squash for 3-4 minutes or until softened and golden. Remove and set aside. Add the onions and garlic to the pan and cook slowly for 10-15 minutes.

3 Spoon the sliced squash, courgettes and tomatoes into an ovenproof dish or tin and top with the onions and garlic, herbs, seasoning and remaining oil. Cover with foil and cook at 200°C (400°F) mark 6 for 15 minutes. Uncover and cook for about 40 minutes until tender.

4 Serve sprinkled with the olives and crumbled cheese.

Freezing: not suitable

Cranberry Chutney

A delicious accompaniment to roast turkey, make this chutney well in advance of Christmas to allow it to mature.

Preparation time: 10 minutes, plus storing
Cooking time: 30 minutes
15 cals per 15 ml (1 tbsp)
Serves 8

700 g (1½ lb) cranberries

300 ml (10 fl oz) distilled malt vinegar

225 g (8 oz) sultanas

125 g (4 oz) seedless raisins

125 g (4 oz) sugar

15 g (½ oz) salt

10 ml (2 tsp) each ground cinnamon and ground allspice

1 Put all the ingredients in a large saucepan. Simmer gently, stirring occasionally, for about 30 minutes or until the mixture has thickened.

2 Pour the chutney into sterilised hot, dry jars. Cover, and seal in the usual way. Leave to mature for one month; store for up to 6 months.

Freezing: not suitable

Prune and Garlic Chutney

This garlicky chutney makes an interesting addition to a turkey-roast meal.

Preparation time: 45 minutes
Cooking time: 2 hours
90 cals per 15 ml (1 tbsp)
Makes about 1.6 kg (3½ lb)

20 garlic cloves, about 2 bulbs

30 ml (2 tbsp) oil

450 g (1 lb) onions

75 g (3 oz) butter

1.4 kg (3 lb) Bramley apples

225 g (8 oz) no-soak pitted dried prunes

grated rind and juice of 1 lemon

450 g (1 lb) demerara sugar

salt and pepper

1 Peel the garlic, put in a small roasting tin and drizzle over the oil. Cook at 200°C (400°F) mark 6 for 40 minutes or until the garlic is soft.

2 Meanwhile, peel and chop the onions. In a preserving pan or stainless-steel saucepan, melt the butter; fry the onions for about 15 minutes until soft and beginning to brown.

3 Peel and core the apples and cut into 2 cm (¾ inch) chunks. Roughly chop the prunes. Mash the garlic. Add the apples, prunes, garlic, juice and rind of the lemon and the sugar to the onions. Stir well, then bring to the boil. Simmer, uncovered, over a low heat for 2 hours or until no excess liquid remains, stirring occasionally. Season with salt and pepper to taste.

4 Pour into sterilised hot, dry jars. Cover and seal in the usual way. Leave to mature for one month. Store for up to 3 months.

Freezing: not suitable

Cranberry and Apple Sauce

Cranberry and Apple Sauce

The sauce can be stored in the refrigerator for up to 5 days. For extra sweetness and texture, add 50 g (2 oz) dried cranberries to the fresh ones.

Preparation time: 15 minutes
Cooking time: 10 minutes
100 cals per serving
Serves 8

2 eating apples

50 g (2 oz) butter

500 g (1 lb 2 oz) cranberries

about 75 g (3 oz) caster sugar

1 Peel, core and dice the apples. Melt the butter in a saucepan. Once foaming, fry the apples over a high heat for 2-3 minutes.

2 Add the cranberries, continue cooking over a moderate heat for 4-5 minutes or until soft. Add 75 g (3 oz) sugar, or to taste, then bubble the sauce for 1-2 minutes.

Freezing: suitable. Thaw at cool room temperature overnight. Cover and reheat gently for 4-5 minutes.

Golden Brandy Sauce

Excellent as an accompaniment to Christmas pudding, this sauce is also wonderful served straight from the freezer like ice cream.

Preparation time: 15 minutes, plus chilling
Cooking time: none
210 cals per serving
Serves 8-10

3 egg yolks

300 ml (10 fl oz) double cream

45 ml (3 tbsp) golden syrup

30 ml (2 tbsp) brandy

1 Beat the yolks until creamy. Whip the cream until it just holds its shape. Warm the syrup very slightly.
2 Mix all the ingredients together. Cover, and chill overnight. Remove from the refrigerator 30 minutes before serving.

Freezing: suitable. Thaw overnight in the refrigerator.

Brandy Butter

The classic accompaniment to Christmas Pudding, this flavoured butter can be made up to 3 days in advance; store in the refrigerator.

Preparation time: 15 minutes, plus chilling
Cooking time: none
195 cals per serving
Serves 8

125 g (4 oz) unsalted butter

125 g (4 oz) soft light brown (muscovado) sugar

90 ml (6 tbsp) brandy

1 Place the unsalted butter in a bowl and beat until it is very soft. Sift the brown sugar and add gradually to the butter, beating well between each addition, until very light and fluffy.
2 Beat in the brandy, spoonful by spoonful, then transfer to a serving bowl and chill for at least 2-3 hours.

Freezing: not suitable

desserts

Mincemeat and Marzipan Tart

Preparation time: 1 hour, plus chilling
Cooking time: 45 minutes
780 cals per serving
Serves 8

225 g (8 oz) plain white flour

pinch of salt

grated rind and juice of ½ orange

150 g (5 oz) butter

2 eggs

250 g (9 oz) white almond marzipan

caster sugar for dusting

300 ml (10 fl oz) double cream, to serve

EXTRA-FRUITY MINCEMEAT

grated rind and juice of 1 lemon

125 g (4 oz) each raisins and sultanas

125 g (4 oz) each currants and dried, ready-to-eat peaches, apricots or pears

1.25 ml (¼ tsp) mixed spice

100 g (3½ oz) soft light brown (muscovado) sugar

100 ml (4 fl oz) brandy

200 g (7 oz) crisp eating apples

125 g (4 oz) seedless white grapes

1 To make the mincemeat, add the lemon rind and juice to the dried fruit with the mixed spice, brown sugar and brandy. Peel the apples and cut the flesh into small cubes. Halve the grapes and stir into the mixture. Cover and set aside in the refrigerator for at least 24 hours.

2 To make the tart, place the flour and salt in a food processor and process for 1-2 seconds. Add the orange rind and butter; process until the mixture resembles fine breadcrumbs. Lightly beat the eggs, mix 30 ml (2 tbsp) with 30 ml (2 tbsp) of the orange juice and set aside remainder. With the machine running, add the egg and orange mixture, then process until the mixture begins to come together. Turn onto a floured work surface and knead lightly until smooth. Chill for 30 minutes.

3 Roll the pastry out thinly to line a 23 cm (9 inch) fluted tart tin. Line with greaseproof paper and baking beans and bake at 200°C (400°F) mark 6 for 15 minutes. Remove the baking beans and paper, then return to the oven for 5 minutes. Brush the pastry with some reserved egg to seal, then return to the oven for 1-2 minutes.

4 Drain the mincemeat, reserving the juice. Cut 50 g (2 oz) of the marzipan into small dice, add to the mincemeat and spoon into the pastry case. Roll the remaining marzipan out thinly; cut into long strips 5 mm (¼ inch) wide. Overlap in a lattice pattern on top of the mincemeat filling. Brush with beaten egg and dust heavily with sugar. Bake for 15-20 minutes or until the marzipan is golden brown. Leave for 10 minutes in the tin. Cool a little on a wire rack.

5 Meanwhile, whip the cream and whisk in the reserved mincemeat juice; serve with the warm tart.

Freezing: suitable at the end of step 4. Cool in the tin; wrap and freeze tart and the mincemeat juice separately. Reheat the tart from frozen at 200°C (400°F) mark 6 for 30-40 minutes. Unmould after 5 minutes. Thaw mincemeat juice at cool room temperature for 3-4 hours. Complete step 5.

Prune, Apple and Calvados Tart

Preparation time: 30 minutes, plus chilling
Cooking time: 50 minutes
685 cals per serving
Serves 8

175 g (6 oz) plain white flour

225 g (8 oz) butter

125 g (4 oz) caster sugar

grated rind and juice of 1 orange

1 egg yolk

225 g (8 oz) pitted no-soak prunes

1 eating apple

60 ml (4 tbsp) Calvados

225 g (8 oz) ground almonds

2 eggs, beaten

25 g (1 oz) slivered or flaked almonds

125 g (4 oz) apricot jam

Greek yogurt or crème fraîche, to serve

1 Put the flour, 125 g (4 oz) diced chilled butter, 25 g (1 oz) caster sugar and the grated orange rind in a food processor. Process until the mixture resembles breadcrumbs. Turn out into a bowl.

2 Mix 30 ml (2 tbsp) water and the egg yolk, blend into the mixture and knead lightly to form a ball. Wrap and chill for about 30 minutes.

3 Roughly chop the prunes, grate the apple and pour over the Calvados. Melt the remaining butter and mix with the ground almonds, the beaten eggs and the remaining caster sugar.

4 Roll the pastry thinly and use to line a 23 cm (9 inch) round, 4 cm (1¼ inch) deep, loose-based, fluted flan tin. Bake blind until set.

5 Add the prunes and apple to the almond mixture and spoon into the flan case. Sprinkle with slivered or flaked almonds and bake at 190°C (375°F) mark 5 for 30 minutes or until lightly browned. Leave to cool for about 20 minutes.

6 Melt the apricot jam with 15 ml (1 tbsp) orange juice. When bubbling, sieve, then brush over the top of the cooked tart. Serve warm or cold with Greek yogurt or crème fraîche.

Freezing: suitable. Open-freeze with glaze. Thaw overnight at cool room temperature. Reheat, loosely covered, for about 20 minutes.

Prune, Apple and Calvados Tart

Chocolate Meringue Roulade

Chocolate Meringue Roulade

It's hard to believe this delicious pudding has so few calories.

Preparation time: 30 minutes, plus cooling
Cooking time: 1 hour
260-195 cals per serving
Serves 6-8

5 egg whites
175 g (6 oz) caster sugar

5 ml (1 tsp) cornflour
60 ml (4 tbsp) half-fat crème fraîche
125 g (4 oz) chocolate spread
50 g (2 oz) cooked, vacuum-packed chestnuts (optional)
icing sugar and cocoa powder, to dust
chocolate shavings, to decorate
half-fat crème fraîche, to serve

1 Use non-stick baking parchment to line a 31.5 x 21.5 cm (12½ x 8½ inch) Swiss-roll tin.

2 With an electric whisk, whisk the egg whites in a large bowl until frothy, then whisk in the sugar. Stand the bowl over a pan of gently simmering water and whisk at high speed for about 4-5 minutes until very thick and shiny. Take off the heat and whisk in the cornflour.

3 Spoon the mixture into the prepared tin and level the surface. Bake at 100°C (200°F) mark ¼ for 1 hour or until just firm on the surface. Cool, uncovered, for 1 hour. (Do not worry if the meringue mixture weeps a little as it cools.)

4 Beat the crème fraîche into the chocolate spread. Roughly chop the chestnuts, if using, and fold in.

5 Lightly dust a sheet of baking parchment with icing sugar. Turn the meringue out onto the paper, upside down. Carefully peel off the parchment. Make a shallow cut on the meringue about 2.5 cm (1 inch) in from the edge of the nearest short end. Spread the chocolate mixture over the meringue and roll it up as you would a Swiss roll, starting from the end with the cut.

6 Dust with a little more icing sugar and cocoa powder and sprinkle over the chocolate shavings. Serve with crème fraîche.

Freezing: suitable at the end of step 5. Thaw at cool room temperature for 2 hours, then decorate and serve.

Cinnamon Custard Tart with Caramelised Fruits

Preparation time: 50 minutes, plus chilling for 1 hour and standing for 20-30 minutes
Cooking time: 1½ hours
655 cals per serving
Serves 8

250 g (9 oz) plain flour, plus extra for dusting

100 g (3½ oz) butter

100 g (3½ oz) icing sugar

4 large eggs

450 ml (¾ pint) milk

248 ml (10 fl oz) carton double cream

1 vanilla pod

1 cinnamon stick

275 g (10 oz) caster sugar

1 mango, 1 small pineapple, 2 clementines and 125 g (4 oz) kumquats, to accompany

1 Place the flour, butter and icing sugar in a food processor and process until the mixture forms fine crumbs. Lightly beat one egg and add to the flour mixture with 15 ml (1 tbsp) water. Process until the crumbs just come together to make a dough. Wrap the pastry in clingfilm and refrigerate for 30 minutes.

2 Roll the pastry out on a lightly floured worksurface and use to line a 23 cm (9 inch) loose-bottomed tart tin. Prick the base well and line with greaseproof paper and baking beans. Refrigerate for 30 minutes. Place on a baking tray and bake at 200°C (400°F) mark 6 for 15 minutes, then remove the paper and baking beans and cook for a further 10-15 minutes until the base of the pastry is cooked. Lightly whisk the remaining eggs. Use 15 ml (1 tbsp) beaten egg to brush over the base and sides of the pastry case to seal, then return to the oven for 2 minutes.

3 Place the milk, cream, split vanilla pod and crumbled cinnamon stick in a large pan. Bring slowly to the boil, then set aside to infuse for 20 minutes. Mix the remaining whisked egg with 150 g (5 oz) sugar. Stir the hot milk into the egg mixture, strain through a fine sieve into a jug and pour into the tart. (It may be easiest to fill the flan case without taking it out of the oven completely. This will prevent the custard spilling as you put it back.)

4 Cook at 150°C (300°F) mark 2 for 40-50 minutes or until the filling has just set in the middle. Turn the oven off and leave the tart in the oven for 15 minutes before taking it out and setting aside to cool. Leave the tart in the tin for 20-30 minutes before carefully transferring to a cooling rack to cool completely.

5 To decorate, cut thick slices of mango, pineapple, clementines and kumquats and spread over two non-stick baking sheets. Place remaining sugar in a small, heavy-based saucepan. Cook over a low heat until the sugar begins to dissolve, turn up the heat and cook to a pale caramel. Cool a little and drizzle over the fruit. Allow to set. Cut the tart into portions and spoon the fruit over the top just before serving.

Freezing: suitable at the end of step 4, cool, pack and freeze. Defrost at cool room temperature overnight. Complete the recipe.

Brandy Snap Coffee Cups

Brandy Snap Coffee Cups

These cups look stunning, but you can spoon the parfait into ready-made brandy snaps or espresso coffee cups if you are short of time.

Preparation time: 1¾ hours, plus chilling
Cooking time: 20 minutes
600 cals per serving
Serves 6

BRANDY SNAP COFFEE CUPS

100g (3½ oz) plain white flour

10 ml (2 tsp) ground ginger

pinch of cream of tartar

100 g (3½ oz) caster sugar

100 g (3½ oz) butter

45 ml (3 tbsp) golden syrup

COFFEE PARFAIT

3 egg yolks

75 g (3 oz) icing sugar

375 g (13 oz) mascarpone cheese

5 ml (1 tsp) vanilla essence

30 ml (2 tbsp) cold strong coffee

15 ml (1 tbsp) rum

CREAM TOPPING

75 ml (3 fl oz) double cream

30 ml (2 tbsp) icing sugar

15 ml (1 tbsp) rum

cocoa powder for dusting

chocolate curls and chocolate-coated espresso beans, to decorate

1 To make the coffee cups you will need one rectangle of greaseproof paper 20.5 x 5 cm (8 x 2 inches), one plain 6.5 cm (2½ inch) cutter, one plain 3 cm (1½ inch) cutter, one 10 cm (4 inch) saucer.

2 For the coffee-cup mixture, sift together the flour, ginger and cream of tartar. Warm the sugar, butter and syrup until the sugar dissolves and the ingredients are blended; stir occasionally. Cool for 1 minute. Add the flour mixture and stir until smooth.

3 To shape the cups and saucers, spread half the brandy snap mixture on a shallow non-stick baking sheet measuring 38 x 28 cm (15 x 11 inches). Bake at 190°C (375°F) mark 5 for 7 minutes or until the mixture has spread over the entire base and is deep golden. Remove from the oven and leave for 1 minute.

4 While still warm, cut out a rectangle with scissors using the greaseproof paper as a template. Quickly curl into a cylinder and place inside the 6.5 cm (2½ inch) cutter for 30 seconds, until set. Remove and cool on a wire rack. Shape five more cups. (If the mixture hardens while shaping, return to the oven for a few minutes to soften.)

5 Spread the rest of the uncooked mixture over the baking sheet. Cook as above. Remove from the oven and leave for 1 minute. While still warm, cut out six discs using the saucer as a template and six circles with the small cutter, for the cup handles. Quickly mould the discs over the saucer to shape. While still warm, slip the small circles between the overlap crease of the cups and gently bend backwards to create a handle. Sit each one on a 'saucer' and chill in the freezer.

6 For coffee parfait, whisk the egg yolks and icing

sugar together for 2 minutes until thick and light in colour. Beat in the mascarpone, vanilla essence, coffee and rum. Freeze for 2 hours or until just frozen.

7 Remove the parfait from the freezer, beat until smooth and divide among the coffee cups. For the topping, whip the cream, icing sugar and rum until just stiff, then spoon some on top of each cup. Freeze for at least 6 hours, preferably overnight.

8 To serve, dust with cocoa and decorate with curls and chocolate-coated espresso beans.

Freezing: suitable at the end of step 7. Remove from freezer to refrigerator 20 minutes before serving, then decorate.

Chocolate and Cherry Amaretti Tart

Chocolate and cherries are a classic combination. The morello cherries used here give a greater depth of flavour.

Preparation time: 30 minutes, plus 50 minutes chilling
Cooking time: 1½ hours, plus cooling
764 cals per serving
Serves 8

400 g (14 oz) pitted morello cherries (bottled or canned), drained

45 ml (3 tbsp) brandy, sloe gin or almond-flavoured liqueur

PASTRY

150 g (5 oz) butter, softened

50 g (2 oz) icing sugar

1 small egg, beaten

225 g (8 oz) plain white flour, sieved, plus extra for dusting

FILLING

100 g (3½ oz) plain chocolate

125 g (4 oz) butter, softened

125 g (4 oz) caster sugar

3 large eggs, beaten

125 g (4 oz) ground almonds

25 g (1 oz) self-raising flour

50 g (2 oz) amaretti biscuits, crushed

75 g (3 oz) slivered or flaked almonds

icing sugar to dust

1 Place the morello cherries in a bowl with the brandy, sloe gin or almond-flavoured liqueur and set aside for 30 minutes to allow the flavours to develop. Meanwhile, make the pastry. Place the butter, icing sugar and egg in a food processor and whizz until almost smooth. Add the flour and process until the mixture just begins to form a dough. On a floured worksurface, lightly knead the pastry, then wrap and chill for 30 minutes.

2 On a lightly floured worksurface, roll out the pastry and line a 24 cm (9½ inch) fluted, loose-bottomed flan tin. Chill for 20 minutes. Line with greaseproof paper and baking beans and cook at 200°C (400°F) mark 6 for 15 minutes. Remove the paper and beans and return to the oven for a further 5 minutes.

3 To make the filling, place the plain chocolate in a heatproof bowl over a pan of simmering water and stir until melted and smooth. Set aside to cool. In a bowl, beat together the butter and sugar until pale and fluffy. Gradually beat in the eggs, alternately with the almonds and flour. Finally, fold in the cooled melted chocolate and amaretti biscuits.

4 Spoon about one-third of the mixture over the base of the pastry case. Spoon the cherries evenly over the surface, then top with the remaining filling mixture and spread out carefully to cover the cherries. Sprinkle the almonds over the top and bake at 150°C (300°F) mark 2 for about 1 hour. The tart will have a thin crust on top but be quite soft underneath.

5 Cool in the tin for 10-15 minutes before unmoulding and dusting with icing sugar. Serve warm.

Freezing: suitable at the end of step 4; cool, wrap and freeze. Thaw at cool room temperature overnight. Warm through as above and dust with icing sugar before serving.

Iced Maple and Ginger Meringue Cake

Preparation time: 30 minutes, plus freezing
Cooking time: 2½ hours
385 cals per serving
Serves 8

175 g (6 oz) mixed walnuts and hazelnuts

5 egg whites

275 g (10 oz) caster sugar

50 g (2 oz) stem ginger

3 whole eggs

60 ml (4 tbsp) maple-flavour syrup

300 ml (10 fl oz) Greek natural yogurt

kumquats, walnuts and icing sugar, to decorate

1 Draw two 20.5 cm (8 inch) circles on non-stick baking parchment. Turn the paper over and place on baking sheets. Brown the nuts under a grill, allow to cool, then roughly chop.
2 Whisk the egg whites with an electric whisk until stiff but not dry. Gradually add half the caster sugar, whisking after each addition until the meringue is stiff and glossy. Fold in the remaining sugar and half the nuts.
3 Spread half the meringue on one paper circle, the other half in an irregular shape on the second circle.
4 Bake at 110°C (225°F) mark ¼ for about 2½ hours. The meringue will weep. Turn off the oven and allow to cool completely. Peel off the paper.
5 Chop the stem ginger. Separate the whole eggs and whisk the yolks and maple-flavour syrup until thick and mousse-like. Fold in the yogurt with the ginger, remaining nuts and the whisked egg whites. Freeze, stirring about every 30 minutes, until the ice is thick enough to sandwich between the meringues. (This will take about 2-2½ hours.)
6 Spread the ice mixture onto the smooth meringue circle and place the irregular one on the top. Freeze for at least 4 hours or until firm.
7 Place in refrigerator for 1½ hours, before slicing. Decorate with kumquats, walnuts and icing sugar.

Freezing: suitable. Open-freeze without decoration; serve as above.

Raspberry and Almond Trifle

Preparation time: 30 minutes, plus chilling
Cooking time: none
725 cals per serving
Serves 6

125 g (4 oz) blanched almonds

450 g (1 lb) fresh or frozen raspberries

finely grated rind and juice of 1 lemon

icing sugar, to taste

225 g (8 oz) ratafias

75 ml (5 tbsp) Amaretto di Saronno, or other almond liqueur

150 ml (5 fl oz) dry Madeira or sherry

freshly grated nutmeg

450 ml (15 fl oz) double cream

gold and silver sugared almonds, silver balls and extra ratafias, to decorate

1 Toast the almonds under the grill or in a moderate oven until evenly golden. Allow to cool, then chop roughly.
2 Purée half of the raspberries in a blender or food processor. Sieve to remove the pips and stir in the lemon juice and icing sugar to taste.
3 Divide the ratafias between individual serving glasses and sprinkle with the toasted almonds and 45 ml (3 tbsp) almond liqueur. Scatter over the whole raspberries and sprinkle with a little icing sugar. Pour over the raspberry purée. Cover and chill in the refrigerator.
4 Meanwhile, put the lemon rind in a bowl with the Madeira or sherry, remaining liqueur and nutmeg. Leave to macerate for at least 1 hour, then strain.
5 Whisk the cream with icing sugar to taste until just beginning to thicken, then gradually whisk in the flavoured wine and liqueur until the mixture holds soft peaks. Spoon over the raspberries and ratafias. Cover and chill for at least 1 hour before serving.
6 Just before serving, decorate with gold and silver sugared almonds, silver balls and extra ratafias.

Freezing: not suitable

Raspberry and Almond Trifle

Zabaglione Ice Cream

This wonderful dessert is smooth and creamy with an irresistible flavour. It needs no stirring while it freezes as the alcohol keeps it soft and whisking keeps it light.

Preparation time: 15 minutes
Cooking time: 30 minutes, plus 30 minutes chilling and overnight freezing
340 cals per serving
Serves 6

50 g (2 oz) caster sugar

4 large egg yolks

250 ml (9 fl oz) double cream

60 ml (4 tbsp) Malmsey Madeira or dark cream sherry

50 g (2 oz) macaroons or ratafias, roughly crushed

25 g (1½ oz) shelled pistachio nuts, chopped

1 Line a 450 g (1 lb) loaf tin with clingfilm or non-stick baking parchment. Put the caster sugar in a small pan with 100 ml (4 fl oz) water and bring slowly to the boil, making sure the sugar is dissolved before boiling. Bubble for 3 minutes.

2 Put the egg yolks in a heatproof bowl and whisk until light and fluffy. Gradually whisk in the hot sugar syrup.

3 Sit the bowl over a pan of barely simmering water with the water just touching the bowl. Cook, stirring, for about 15 minutes or until the mixture is thickened and coats the back of the spoon. Be careful the mixture doesn't get too hot or the eggs will scramble.

4 Remove the bowl from the heat and, using an electric whisk, whisk for 10 minutes or until the mixture is thick, glossy, cold and almost doubled in volume. Cover and chill for 30 minutes.

5 Whisk the cream with the Malmsey until it holds soft peaks. Carefully fold into the chilled egg mixture. Spoon into the prepared tin and freeze overnight.

6 Just before serving, turn the ice cream out onto a chilled serving dish, peel away the clingfilm and gently press the mixed macaroons and pistachios over the top and the long sides. Cut into slices and serve.

Freezing: suitable at the end of step 5. To use, complete the recipe.

Sloe Gin Jelly

An unusual and alcoholic pudding that's sure to be a hit with your guests.

Preparation time: 30 minutes, plus marinating for 2 hours or overnight and chilling
Cooking time: 15 minutes
225-170 cals per serving
Serves 6-8

350 g (12 oz) small black seedless grapes

300 ml (½ pint) sloe gin

125 g (4 oz) kumquats

10 ml (2 level tsp) powdered gelatine

75g (3 oz) granulated sugar

1 Lightly prick the grapes with a cocktail stick and place in a bowl. Reserve 60 ml (4 tbsp) sloe gin and pour the remainder over the grapes; cover and refrigerate for at least 2 hours or overnight.

2 Slice the kumquats. Place the reserved 60 ml (4 tbsp) sloe gin in a bowl, sprinkle powdered gelatine over and leave to soak for 5 minutes.

3 Place 600 ml (1 pint) water in a saucepan, add the sugar and cook over a low heat until the sugar has dissolved. Bring to the boil and bubble until the liquid has reduced by half, then leave to cool for 1 minute. Add the soaked gelatine, then stir until melted.

4 Add the macerated grapes and their liquid to the syrup with kumquats and stir until well mixed. Place in a bowl and refrigerate until the jelly begins to set (about 1 hour).

5 Spoon jelly into six or eight champagne flutes, then cover and refrigerate for 1 hour or until set.

6 Take the jellies out of the fridge about 30-45 minutes before serving to allow the jelly to soften slightly.

Freezing: not suitable

baking

Star Cake

Bake ahead for Christmas with this especially moist, tropical fruit-packed cake, which is delicious served simply as it is, or topped with white marzipan and fondant icing.

Preparation time: 40 minutes, plus soaking
Cooking time: 2½ hours
560 cals per serving (cake only)
980 cals per serving (decorated)
Serves 10

125 g (4 oz) no-soak dried apricots

175 g (6 oz) medjool dates, stoned

75 g (3 oz) dried pineapple

75 g (3 oz) dried papaya

75 g (3 oz) dried mango

50 g (2 oz) dried cherries

50 g (2 oz) dried cranberries

75 g (3 oz) crystallised ginger

175 g (6 oz) raisins

200 ml (7 fl oz) ginger wine

melted butter for greasing

125 g (4 oz) brazil nuts

1 apple

grated rind and juice of 1 small lemon

200 g (7 oz) self-raising flour

2.5 ml (½ tsp) ground mixed spice

2.5 ml (½ tsp) ground cinnamon

2.5 ml (½ tsp) ground nutmeg

2.5 ml (½ tsp) ground cloves

2.5 ml (½ tsp) salt

200 g (7 oz) butter, softened

75 g (3 oz) demerara sugar

75 g (3 oz) black treacle

3 eggs, beaten

1 Roughly chop any large pieces of dried fruit. Place all the fruit in a bowl and stir in 100 ml (4 fl oz) ginger wine. Cover and leave overnight.

2 Grease a 20.5 cm (8 inch) round, deep cake tin. Cut two circles of greaseproof paper to fit the base of the tin. Cut out a sheet of greaseproof paper large enough to go around the circumference of the tin and three times its height. Fold in half and turn up a 2.5 cm (1 inch) rim along the folded edge. Snip into the rim at intervals. Line the base of the tin with one of the circles. Grease, then line the side of the tin with the strip of paper, the snipped edge resting on the base. Grease again. Place the remaining circle on top.

3 Roughly chop the brazil nuts and set aside. Peel, quarter and core the apple. Coarsely grate the flesh and combine with the lemon rind and juice.

4 Sift the flour, ground spices and salt into a bowl.

5 With an electric whisk or beater, combine the butter with the demerara sugar and black treacle until the mixture turns paler. With the machine still running, gradually add the eggs. Fold in the sifted flour, the grated apple mixture, nuts and soaked fruit.

6 Spoon into the prepared tin and level the top. Bake at 150°C (300°F) mark 2 for about 2½ hours. Cover with foil for the last 20 minutes if necessary.

7 Remove from the oven and leave to cool in the tin. Pierce the cake with a skewer and drizzle over the remaining ginger wine. Wrap in greaseproof paper then tightly in cling film. Store in a cool, dry place for up to 6 weeks.

TO MARZIPAN

Warm 30-45 ml (2-3 tbsp) honey or sieved apricot jam with 15 ml (1 tbsp) water and brush over the cake. On a surface lightly dusted with icing sugar, roll out about 250 g (9 oz) white marzipan to a circle the same size as the cake top. Place on top of the cake and trim off the excess. Roll out another 250 g (9 oz) marzipan to a rectangle about 30.5 x 11.5 cm (12 x 4½ inches). Trim the edges and cut into 2 pieces lengthways. Fit onto the sides of the cake and smooth the joins. Leave, covered with greaseproof paper, in a dry place for one week before icing.

TO MAKE FONDANT STARS

Knead 450 g (1 lb) fondant icing on a surface dusted with icing sugar until pliable. Knead in 5 ml (1 tsp) gum tragacanth, which helps the fondant harden. Roll the icing out to a thickness of 3 mm (⅛ inch). Using a cutter, stamp out 40 stars and transfer to a baking sheet lined with non-stick baking parchment. Brush the stars sparingly with a sugar and water solution and press edible gold leaf onto their surface, or decorate the tips of the stars with gold

Star Cake

and silver balls. Place the stars on a baking sheet and leave in a dry, warm place for at least 24 hours to dry and harden.

TO FONDANT-ICE

Warm 30-45 ml (2-3 tbsp) honey or sieved apricot jam with 15 ml (1 tbsp) water. Brush over the marzipan. On a surface lightly dusted with icing sugar, roll out 450 g (1 lb) ready-to-roll fondant icing to a round about 12.5 cm (5 inches) larger than the cake top. Place on top of the cake and press down the sides. Trim the base. Leave to dry in a cool place, covered with greaseproof paper for 24 hours. Push the fondant stars into the cake at angles and tie a ribbon round.

Jewelled Christmas Cake

A simple topping of glacé fruit turns this rich, moist fruit cake into a dazzling Christmas treat.

Preparation time: 1 hour, plus standing
Cooking time: about 3½ hours
725 cals per serving
Serves 10

125 g (4 oz) glacé cherries

50 g (2 oz) no-soak dried apricots

225 g (8 oz) each currants, sultanas and seedless raisins

50 g (2 oz) chopped mixed peel

100 ml (4 fl oz) brandy

melted butter for greasing

50 g (2 oz) blanched, skinned almonds

50 g (2 oz) Brazil nuts

225 g (8 oz) butter

finely grated rind of 1 lemon

225 g (8 oz) soft dark brown sugar

4 eggs

225 g (8 oz) plain white flour

5 ml (1 tsp) ground mixed spice

2.5 ml (½ tsp) ground cinnamon

1.25 ml (¼ tsp) ground mace

30 ml (2 tbsp) milk

120 ml (8 tbsp) apricot jam

selection of glacé fruit, to decorate

1 Rinse the cherries under cold water to remove the syrup. Drain well and dry on kitchen paper. Cut into quarters. Roughly chop the apricots. Place the cherries, apricots and remaining dried fruit and mixed peel in a bowl. Pour over 75 ml (3 fl oz) brandy, stirring well. Cover and leave to stand overnight. Roughly chop all the nuts and cover tightly.

2 Grease a 20.5 cm (8 inch) round, deep cake tin. Cut two circles of greaseproof paper to fit the base of the tin. Cut out a sheet of greaseproof paper large enough to go around the circumference of the tin and three times its height. Fold in half and turn up a 2.5 cm (1 inch) rim along the folded edge. Snip into the rim at intervals. Line the base of the tin with one of the circles. Grease, then line the side of the tin with the strip of paper, the snipped edge resting on the base. Grease again. Place the remaining circle on top.

3 Using an electric whisk, beat the butter with the grated lemon rind until soft and pale. Gradually beat in the dark brown sugar until blended. In a jug, lightly whisk the eggs, then slowly beat into the creamed ingredients. The mixture should have a smooth consistency after each addition of whisked egg.

4 Sift together the flour, ground mixed spice, cinnamon and mace. Using a large metal spoon, gently fold the flour into the creamed ingredients, along with the soaked fruit, nuts and milk. (Don't be tempted to beat the ingredients in at this stage or the cake mixture will become tough.) Spoon into the prepared cake tin and level the surface.

5 Tie a double band of brown paper around the outside of the tin. Place a double sheet of brown paper on the middle oven shelf and sit the cake tin on top. Bake at 150°C (300°F) mark 2 for about 3½ hours or until a skewer inserted in the centre of the cake comes out quite clean. (If necessary, cover lightly with foil to prevent over-browning.) Leave to cool in the tin.

6 Skewer the surface of the cake, spoon over the remaining brandy and leave it to soak in. Turn the cake out and wrap it in greaseproof paper and foil. Store in a cool, dry place for up to 3 months.

7 To complete, place the cake on a board. Heat the jam with 15 ml (1 tbsp) water, then sieve and cool slightly. Brush the cake with the glaze; top with glacé fruit and glaze again. Decorate with ribbon. Cover with a foil tent and store in a cool place for up to one week.

Freezing: not suitable

QUICK DECORATING IDEAS FOR A CHRISTMAS CAKE

1 PRETTY PRESENTS

Marzipan and ice a fruit cake. Wrap striped ribbon and gold ribbon around the sides of the cake. Secure with icing or pins. Wrap foil-wrapped chocolates in coloured gift wrap and tie each one with thin purple ribbon. Pile the chocolates on top of the cake and scatter top and base with tropical-fruit sweets. Tie a large bow with matching ribbon and secure on the top.

2 HEAVENLY SPIRIT

Marzipan and ice a fruit cake. Cut strips from sheet music and glue lengths of braid and tassels onto each end. Wrap a length of black and gold ribbon around the cake and secure with icing or pins. Fix a piece of braid around the base with icing. Finish the musical theme with three gold cherubs. Place the cake on a board, wrapped in gold paper, if wished.

3 WINTER WREATH

Buy or make a wreath, using artificial fir, pine cones, mini Christmas parcels and small artificial apples. If wished, make the wreath edible, using kumquats, nuts and cinnamon sticks. Place over an iced fruit cake – the wreath should fit comfortably around it. Decorate the top with candies and use the decorated cake as a table centrepiece.

4 A MASS OF MARBLES

Marzipan a fruit cake. Fondant-ice the cake and base. Knot a ribbon or piece of soft fabric at regular intervals; attach to the cake with icing or pins. Wrap clear boiled sweets in cellophane and secure four on top of the cake. Pile in the centre of the cake and tumbling over the edges.

5 BLUE PLANET

Marzipan a fruit cake. Mix a few drops of blue food colouring into 450 g (1 lb) ready-to-roll icing and ice the cake. Roll out a further 225 g (8 oz) icing and cut out a moon. Using cutters, stamp out stars; brush cake with water and press stars on. Sprinkle with edible glitter flakes, and scatter blue and clear nuggets around the base, if wished.

6 HIDDEN SURPRISE

Marzipan and ice a fruit cake. Tie gold ribbon and mauve and green striped ribbon around the base and across the top of the cake, then secure with icing or pins. Tie a flamboyant shot-purple ribbon on top.

Pannetone

This classic Italian favourite is really a cross between a bread and a cake, and, because of the high butter content, it keeps well. Pannetone is normally eaten with coffee, or a glass of dessert or fortified wine.

Preparation time: 25 minutes, plus rising
Cooking time: 35 minutes
415-320 cals per serving
Makes 10-12 slices

15 ml (1 tbsp) active dried yeast

150 ml (5 fl oz) warm milk

450 g (1 lb) strong plain white flour

1 egg

4 egg yolks

10 ml (2 tsp) salt

75 g (3 oz) caster sugar

finely grated rind of 1 lemon

finely grated rind of 1 orange

175 g (6 oz) unsalted butter, softened

75 g (3 oz) chopped mixed candied orange and citron peel

125 g (4 oz) raisins

1 Line a 15 cm (6 inch) deep cake tin with a double layer of non-stick baking parchment which projects 12 cm (5 inches) above the rim.

2 Dissolve the yeast in 60 ml (4 tbsp) warm milk. Cover and leave in a warm place for 10 minutes until frothy. Stir in 125 g (4 oz) flour and the remaining warm milk. Cover and leave to rise for 30 minutes.

3 Beat the egg and egg yolks together. Sift the remaining flour and salt onto the yeast mixture. Make a well in the centre and add the sugar, beaten eggs and citrus rinds. Mix to an elastic dough, adding a little more flour if necessary, but keeping the dough quite soft. Work in the softened butter.

4 Cover and leave to rise at room temperature for 2-4 hours until doubled in volume. Meanwhile, chop the candied peel.

5 Knock the dough down and knead in the chopped peel and raisins. Place in the prepared tin and cut an X on the top with a scalpel or very sharp knife. Cover and leave to rise until the dough is about 2.5 cm (1 inch) above the top of the cake tin.

6 Bake at 200°C (400°F) mark 6 for 15 minutes, then lower the heat to 180°C (350°F) mark 4 and bake for a further 40 minutes until well risen and golden. Leave in the tin for 10 minutes, then transfer to a wire rack to cool.

7 Serve cut into horizontal slices. To store, replace the top and wrap the whole pannetone in cling film or foil. Keep in the refrigerator. Bring to room temperature to serve.

Freezing: suitable. Thaw overnight at cool room temperature.

Chocolate and Orange Cake

Preparation time: 25 minutes
Cooking time: 1 hour 40 minutes
495 cals per serving
Serves 16

oil for greasing

125 g (4 oz) white chocolate

125 g (4 oz) milk chocolate

375 g (13 oz) plain chocolate

175 g (6 oz) softened butter

175 g (6 oz) caster sugar

175 g (6 oz) ground almonds

6 eggs, separated

75 g (3 oz) fresh brown breadcrumbs

45 ml (3 tbsp) cocoa powder

grated rind and juice of 1 orange

pinch salt

150 ml (5 fl oz) double cream

1 Grease and line a 20.5 cm (8 inch) base-measurement deep cake tin. Roughly chop the white and milk chocolate and set aside.

2 Break 225 g (8 oz) plain chocolate into a bowl and melt over a pan of gently simmering water; cool slightly.

3 Beat the butter and sugar until light and fluffy. Stir in the melted plain chocolate with the ground almonds, egg yolks, breadcrumbs, cocoa powder and grated rind and juice of the orange.

4 Whisk the egg whites and salt to form soft peaks. Stir a quarter into the chocolate mixture; fold in the remainder with the chopped chocolate.

5 Pour into the prepared tin and bake at 180°C (350°F) mark 4 for about 1 hour 40 minutes, covering loosely with foil if necessary. Cool in the tin for 15 minutes before turning out onto a wire rack.

6 Place the remaining 150 g (5 oz) plain chocolate and cream in a bowl. Melt over a pan of gently simmering water, stirring occasionally. Cool for about 30 minutes or until slightly thickened. Pour over the cake to cover. Cool and store in an airtight container for up to 5 days.

Freezing: suitable at end of step 5. Thaw, wrapped, for 5 hours then complete as above.

Chocolate and Orange Cake

Bûche de Noël

Bûche de Noël is traditionally eaten in France at Christmas time. This and the English Yule Log date back to the days when a huge log used to be burnt on Christmas Eve.

Preparation time: 45 minutes, plus cooling
Cooking time: 10 minutes
720 cals per serving
Makes about 8 slices

oil for greasing
125 g (4 oz) caster sugar, plus extra for dredging
75 g (3 oz) plain flour, plus extra for dredging
3 eggs
30 ml (2 tbsp) cocoa powder
440 g (15½ oz) can sweetened chestnut purée
icing sugar, for dusting
holly sprigs, to decorate

BUTTER CREAM
225 g (8 oz) unsalted butter, softened
50 g (2 oz) plain chocolate
450 g (1 lb) icing sugar

1 To make the cake, grease a 33 x 23 cm (13 x 9 inch) Swiss-roll tin. Line with greaseproof paper and grease the paper. Dredge with a little caster sugar, then with a little flour, knocking out any excess.

2 Put the eggs and sugar in a deep heatproof bowl and stand over a saucepan of simmering water. Whisk until thick enough to leave a trail on the surface when the whisk is lifted. Do not overheat the mixture by letting the bowl come into contact with the simmering water or by having the heat under the saucepan too high.

3 Take the bowl off the saucepan and continue whisking the mixture for 5 minutes or until cool. Sift in the flour and cocoa and gently fold into the mixture. Fold in 15 ml (1 tbsp) hot water.

4 Pour the mixture gently into the prepared tin and lightly level the surface. Bake in the oven at 200°C (400°F) mark 6 for about 10 minutes or until slightly shrunk away from the sides of the tin.

5 Meanwhile, place a sheet of greaseproof paper on top

of a tea-towel. Dredge the paper with caster sugar and turn the cake out onto it. Trim off the crusty edges with a sharp knife. Roll up the cake with the paper inside. Transfer to a wire rack, seam-side down, and leave to cool for 20 minutes.

6 To make the butter cream, beat the butter until soft. Melt the chocolate with 15 ml (1 tbsp) water in a bowl set over a pan of simmering water, then leave to cool slightly. Gradually sift and beat the icing sugar into the softened butter, then add the melted chocolate.

7 Unroll the cold Swiss roll and spread the chestnut purée over the surface. Roll up again without the paper inside. Place on a cake board or plate.

8 Cut a thick diagonal slice off one end of the Swiss roll and attach with butter cream to the side of the roll.

9 Using a piping bag and a large star nozzle, pipe thin lines of butter cream over the log. Pipe one or two swirls of butter cream to represent knots in the wood. Decorate with sprigs of holly and dust lightly with icing sugar.

Freezing: not suitable

Date and Ginger Cake

Make this sticky cake up to one week ahead and store in a tin or in the freezer.

Preparation time: 20 minutes
Cooking time: about 1 hour
210 cals per serving
Makes about 16 slices

oil for greasing
125 g (4 oz) stoned dates
50 g (2 oz) stem ginger in syrup
2.5 ml (½ tsp) bicarbonate of soda
50 ml (2 fl oz) milk
125 g (4 oz) butter
125 g (4 oz) light soft brown (muscovado) sugar
2 eggs
150 g (5 oz) golden syrup
150 g (5 oz) black treacle

225 g (8 oz) plain flour

7.5 ml (1½ tsp) ground ginger

salt

1 Grease and line a 23 cm (9 inch) square cake tin with non-stick baking parchment. Roughly chop the dates and stem ginger. Stir the bicarbonate of soda into the milk.

2 Beat together the butter and sugar until pale and light. Slowly add the beaten eggs and then stir in the syrup, treacle, milk, chopped dates and stem ginger.

3 Fold in the sifted flour, ground ginger and a pinch of salt. Pour into the tin and bake at 150°C (300°F) mark 2 for 1 hour or until a skewer inserted into the cake comes out clean. Leave the cake in the tin for 1 hour. Turn out onto a wire rack.

4 When cool, wrap in greaseproof paper and store.

Freezing: suitable. Thaw overnight at cool room temperature.

Old-time Mince Pies

Preparation time: 30 minutes
Cooking time: 25 minutes
105 cals per mince pie
Makes 24

125 g (4 oz) butter

225 g (8 oz) plain white flour

about 225 g (8 oz) Spicy Apple Mincemeat (see page 185)

1 egg white, lightly beaten

caster sugar for dusting

cream, to accompany

1 Rub the butter into the flour and bind to form a firm dough with about 60 ml (4 tbsp) water. Knead lightly until just smooth. Roll out the pastry thinly and, using a 5.5 cm (2¼ inch) round cutter, cut out about 48 rounds, re-rolling as necessary.

2 Place half the rounds on baking sheets and spoon

Old-time Mince Pies

mincemeat onto the centre of each. Moisten the pastry edges. Cover with the remaining pastry rounds, sealing the edges well; flute, if wished. Make a tiny hole in the top to allow the air to escape.

3 Bake at 200°C (400°F) mark 6 for about 15 minutes or until just set but not browned.

4 Take the pies out of the oven and brush with lightly beaten egg white and dust with caster sugar. Return to the oven for a further 8-10 minutes or until well browned. Serve the mince pies warm with cream.

Freezing: suitable. Thaw overnight at cool room temperature. Refresh in a hot oven for 5 minutes before serving.

Christmas
Morning Muffins

Christmas Morning Muffins

Moist muffins bursting with cranberries make a wonderful start to the celebrations! Have all the dry ingredients mixed together, and prepare the muffin tin the night before. On Christmas morning, just stir in the liquids and cranberries, fill the tins and bake. Serve from the oven – these muffins do not reheat well.

Preparation time: 15 minutes
Cooking time: 20 minutes
175 cals per muffin
Makes 12

175 g (6 oz) fresh cranberries

50 g (2 oz) icing sugar, sifted

150 g (5 oz) plain wholemeal flour

150 g (5 oz) plain white flour

15 ml (1 tbsp) baking powder

5 ml (1 tsp) ground mixed spice

2.5 ml (½ tsp) salt

50 g (2 oz) soft light brown (muscovado) sugar

1 egg

250 ml (8 fl oz) milk

50 ml (2 fl oz) vegetable oil

1 Halve the cranberries and place in a bowl with the icing sugar. Toss gently to mix.

2 Line a twelve-cup muffin tin with paper cases or simply grease with butter. Sift together the flours, baking powder, mixed spice, salt and brown sugar into a large bowl. Make a well in the centre.

3 Beat the egg with the milk and oil. Add to the dry ingredients and stir just until blended, then lightly and quickly stir in the cranberries. The mixture should look roughly mixed, with lumps and floury pockets.

4 Two-thirds fill the muffin cups with the mixture. Bake in the oven at 180°C (350°F) mark 4 for about 20 minutes or until well risen and golden brown.

5 Transfer the muffins to a wire rack to cool slightly. Serve warm.

Freezing: not suitable

VARIATION

Substitute 225 g (8 oz) mincemeat for the cranberries. Add to the well in the middle of the dry ingredients with the liquid. Stir until just moistened but still lumpy. Fill the muffin tins and bake as above.

edible gifts

Florentines

These enticing chewy morsels are rich with fruit and nuts, and this original version also includes sunflower seeds. Pack them in a box, layered with greaseproof paper, for a special gift.

Preparation time: 15 minutes
Cooking time: 8-10 minutes
170 cals per biscuit
Makes 12

oil for greasing

25 g (1 oz) glacé cherries

40 g (1½ oz) flaked almonds

60 g (2½ oz) unsalted butter

50 g (2 oz) caster sugar

30 ml (2 tbsp) double cream

25 g (1 oz) sunflower seeds

20 g (¾ oz) chopped mixed peel

20 g (¾ oz) sultanas

15 g (½ oz) plain white flour

125 g (4 oz) plain dark chocolate, in pieces

1 Lightly grease a large baking sheet. Roughly chop the cherries. Lightly crush the almonds.

2 Melt the butter in a small saucepan. Add the sugar and heat gently until dissolved, then bring to the boil. Remove from the heat and stir in the cream, sunflower seeds, mixed peel, sultanas, cherries, almonds and flour. Beat well until evenly combined.

3 Place heaped teaspoonfuls of the mixture onto the baking sheet, spacing them well apart to allow room for spreading. (You'll probably need to cook half the mixture at a time.)

4 Bake at 180°C (350°F) mark 4 for about 6-8 minutes until the biscuits have spread considerably and the edges are golden brown. Remove from the oven and, using a large plain metal biscuit cutter, push the edges into the centre to create neat rounds. Return to the oven for a further 2 minutes or until deep golden.

5 Leave the Florentines on the baking sheet for 2 minutes to cool slightly, then transfer to a wire rack to cool completely. Cook the remaining mixture in the same way.

6 Melt the chocolate in a heatproof bowl over a pan of simmering water. Stir until smooth. Roll the edges of the biscuits in the chocolate and place on a sheet of non-stick baking parchment until set. Store in an airtight tin.

Freezing: not suitable

VARIATION

For added colour, dip half the biscuits in plain chocolate and the other half in milk or white chocolate.

Shortbread

Shortbread is a traditional Scottish festive bake and no home north of the Border is complete without a home-made yuletide batch. A box or tin of shortbread also makes an ideal gift, especially if you include one or two of the variations suggested on page 181.

Preparation time: 20 minutes, plus chilling
Cooking time: 20 minutes
270-180 cals per biscuit
Makes 24-36

450 g (1 lb) butter

225 g (8 oz) caster sugar

450 g (1 lb) plain white flour

225 g (8 oz) ground rice or rice flour

pinch of salt

golden or coloured granulated sugar for coating

caster sugar, for sprinkling

1 Line 2 baking sheets with greaseproof paper. Make sure all the ingredients are at room temperature. Cream the butter and sugar together in a bowl until pale and fluffy. Sift the flour, rice flour and salt together and stir into the creamed mixture, using a wooden spoon, until it resembles breadcrumbs.

2 Gather the dough together with your hand and turn onto a clean work surface. Knead lightly until it forms a ball, then lightly roll into a sausage, about 5-7.5 cm (2-3 inches) thick. Wrap in cling film and chill until firm.

3 Unwrap the roll and slice into discs, about 7-10 mm (⅓-½ inch) thick. Pour golden or coloured granulated sugar onto a plate and roll the edge of each disc in the sugar. Place the biscuits, cut-side up, on the baking sheets.

4 Bake at 190°C (375°F) mark 5 for about 15-25 minutes, depending on thickness, until very pale golden. Remove from the oven and sprinkle with caster sugar. Allow the shortbread to cool on the baking sheet for 10 minutes, then transfer to a wire rack to cool. Pack into a tin box when cold.

Freezing: not suitable

VARIATIONS

Spiced Shortbread: Sift 15 ml (1 tbsp) ground mixed spice with the flours.

Ginger Shortbread: Sift 5 ml (1 tsp) ground ginger with the flours. Add 50 g (2 oz) chopped crystallised ginger to the dough.

Chocolate Chip Shortbread: Knead 50 g (2 oz) chocolate chips into the dough.

Lavender Shortbread: Add the flowers from 6 lavender heads to the dough. Roll out the dough very thinly and cut into rounds with a biscuit cutter. Bake for 15 minutes only.

Rosemary Shortbread: Add 10 ml (2 tsp) chopped fresh rosemary to the dough. Roll out thinly and bake as for Lavender Shortbread.

Shortbread

Gingerbread Tree Decorations

Fun to make and to give to friends, these little biscuits look lovely hanging on a Christmas tree. You can always decorate them with glacé or royal icing.

Preparation time: 30 minutes, plus cooling
Cooking time: 10 minutes
125 cals per biscuit
Makes about 25

350 g (12 oz) plain white flour

5 ml (1 tsp) bicarbonate of soda

30 ml (2 tbsp) ground ginger

15 ml (1 tbsp) ground cinnamon

2.5 ml (½ tsp) ground cloves

125 g (4 oz) butter

175 g (6 oz) soft light brown (muscovado) sugar

60 ml (4 tbsp) golden syrup

1 egg, size 4

ICING

1 egg white

sifted icing sugar

food colouring

1 Line 2 baking sheets with non-stick baking parchment.
2 Sift the flour with the bicarbonate of soda and spices into a large bowl. Rub in the butter until the mixture resembles fine breadcrumbs. Stir in the sugar.
3 Warm the syrup very slightly and beat in the egg. Cool slightly, the pour onto the flour mixture. Beat with a wooden spoon to a soft dough. Bring together with your hands and knead until smooth.
4 Roll out the mixture on a lightly floured surface to a 5 mm (¼ inch) thickness and cut out shapes with cutters. Make a small hole in the top of each one to enable ribbon to be threaded through after baking.
5 Carefully transfer the shapes to the baking sheets and bake at 190°C (375°F) mark 5 for 8-10 minutes or until golden brown. Leave to cool and harden for 10 minutes on the baking sheet, then transfer to a wire rack to cool completely.

6 To make the icing, beat the egg white until frothy and gradually add enough sifted icing sugar to make a stiff coating or piping consistency. Colour the icing as required.
7 Pipe the icing in patterns over the biscuits and leave to dry. Thread ribbon through the holes in the biscuits in readiness for hanging on the tree.

Freezing: suitable at the end of step 5. Thaw at room temperature for about 2 hours.

Chocolate Truffles

These luscious liqueur-laced bitter chocolate truffles make lovely gifts. They are either covered with a chocolate coating, or simply rolled in cocoa powder, chopped nuts, coconut or grated chocolate. As the texture is a little soft at room temperature rolled truffles, in particular, should be stored in the refrigerator.

Preparation time: 30 minutes-1 hour, plus chilling (and overnight freezing for dipped truffles)
Cooking time: none
65 cals per truffle
Makes about 24

BASIC MIXTURE
225 g (8 oz) quality bitter, plain or milk chocolate

75 ml (3 fl oz) double cream

45 ml (3 tbsp) brandy, rum, orange liqueur, coffee liqueur, coconut liqueur, or vanilla essence

UNDIPPED TRUFFLES

cocoa powder, chopped nuts, dessicated or grated coconut, chocolate vermicelli or grated chocolate, for rolling

DIPPED TRUFFLES

350 g (12 oz) quality plain, milk or white chocolate (or a combination of all three), in small pieces

1 To prepare the basic truffle mixture, grate the chocolate into a small bowl and add the cream. Stand the bowl over a pan of simmering water. Heat very gently until the chocolate begins to melt. Stir well until smooth and remove from the heat. Leave to cool for about 20-30 minutes to room temperature; the mixture should have thickened considerably.

2 Beat in the brandy, rum, liqueur or vanilla. Using an electric whisk, beat for about 5 minutes until the mixture is light, fluffy and paler in colour. It should be firm enough to stand in peaks. Spoon into a shallow tin, cover and refrigerate for at least 2 hours until quite firm.

3 To make simple rolled truffles, sprinkle a tray with cocoa powder and place even-sized teaspoonfuls of truffle mixture on the tray. Dust your hands with a little cocoa powder and quickly roll the mixture into uneven balls. If preferred, roll the truffles in chopped nuts, coconut, chocolate vermicelli or grated chocolate. Place on waxed paper and refrigerate for at least 2 hours.

4 To make dipped truffles, roll the truffle mixture into neat 2.5 cm (1 inch) balls and place on a tray lined with waxed paper. Freeze overnight until rock hard.

5 Melt the chocolate for dipping over simmering water. Check the temperature with a sugar thermometer if possible: it should be 46-49°C (115°-120°F), or 43°C (110°F) for white chocolate.

6 Remove a few truffles at a time from the freezer. Spear each one with a cocktail stick and dip quickly into the chocolate. Shake off excess and place on a tray lined with non-stick baking parchment. Place in the refrigerator for at least 2 hours to set. Repeat with remaining truffles.

7 Place the truffles in paper cases and pack in boxes. Store in the refrigerator for up to 10 days.

Freezing: suitable. Open freeze, then pack in a box. Thaw in refrigerator.

VARIATIONS

Pipe a contrasting colour of chocolate over the dipped truffles or apply a little edible gold leaf, to decorate. Alternatively, press a toasted flaked nut, sliver of crystallised ginger, or a quartered cherry onto the setting chocolate.

Chocolate Truffles

Chocolate Marzipan Pecans

Laced with brandy and the bitter-sweet flavour of cocoa, these pecan-flavoured marzipan sweets are easy to make, yet smart enough to give as gifts. Whole pecans and smooth milk chocolate add the finishing touch, although plain or bitter chocolate could be substituted for a less sweet variation.

Preparation time: 20 minutes, plus standing
Cooking time: none
95 cals per sweet
Makes 20

125 g (4 oz) shelled pecan nuts

40 g (1½ oz) caster sugar

40 g (1½ oz) icing sugar

15 ml (1 tbsp) cocoa powder

10 ml (2 tsp) brandy

1 egg white

75 g (3 oz) milk chocolate

20 shelled pecan nuts, about 40 g (1½ oz), to decorate

1 Put the pecans in a food processor or blender and work to the consistency of ground almonds. Transfer to a bowl and add the caster sugar, icing sugar and cocoa powder. Stir until evenly combined, then mix in the brandy.

2 Beat the egg white lightly with a fork, and add 15 ml (1 tbsp) to the pecan mixture. Mix to a paste, adding a little more egg white if the mixture is too dry.

3 Lightly knead the paste and shape into a cylindrical log, about 3 cm (1¼ inches) thick. Slice the log width-ways into 20 even-sized pieces.

4 Break up the chocolate and melt in a heatproof bowl set over a pan of simmering water. Using a teaspoon, spoon a little melted chocolate onto each sweet and top with a pecan half.

5 Transfer the sweets to a serving plate and store in a cool place for up to 1 week.

Freezing: not suitable

VARIATIONS

Use walnuts or brazil nuts instead of the pecans. Replace the brandy with orange or coffee-flavoured liqueur.

Irish Coffee Cups

Miniature petit four cases make perfect moulds for shaping small chocolates. These delicate chocolate cups cleverly conceal two complimentary layers: one smooth, white and creamy; the other fudge-like and flavoured with coffee and brandy.

Preparation time: 40 minutes, plus setting
Cooking time: none
100 cals per cup
Makes 22

175 g (6 oz) plain chocolate

40 g (1½ oz) white chocolate, to decorate

FILLING

75 g (3 oz) white chocolate

50 ml (2 fl oz) double cream

75 g (3 oz) plain chocolate

10 ml (2 tsp) finely ground espresso coffee

15 ml (1 tbsp) brandy

1 To make the cases, break up 125 g (4 oz) of the plain chocolate and melt in a heatproof bowl set over a pan of simmering water. Separate 20 small foil or paper petit four cases. (Use double thickness paper cases to make coating easier).

2 Spoon a little chocolate into a case and spread evenly over the base and around the sides, using the back of a teaspoon. Invert onto a greaseproof paper lined tray. Coat the remaining cases in the same way and leave in a cool place to set. Turn the set cases the right way up.

3 To make the filling, break up the white chocolate and place in a small saucepan with the cream. Heat gently until the chocolate has melted. Remove from the heat and beat lightly. Use the cream mixture to half-fill the chocolate cases. (Make sure the filling mixtures are not too warm when you fill the cases, otherwise they may melt the cases.)

4 Break up the plain chocolate and melt in a separate bowl. Mix the coffee with 15 ml (1 tbsp) hot water. Add to the melted chocolate with the brandy and stir until smooth. Carefully spoon over the white chocolate until only the rim of the chocolate case remains visible above the level of the plain chocolate and brandy filling.

5 Melt the remaining 50 g (2 oz) plain chocolate for the cases as above. Melt the white chocolate for decoration, place in a greaseproof piping bag and snip off the tip.

6 Spread a little plain chocolate on the surface of one of the cups. Pipe a little white chocolate on top and immediately feather, using a cocktail stick. Repeat on the remaining cups. Store in a cool place for up to 2 weeks.

Freezing: not suitable

Irish Coffee Cups

Spicy Apple Mincemeat

A jar of home-made mincemeat makes a delightful traditional Christmas gift. Attach a circle of gingham fabric to the top of the jar with an elastic band and decorate with ribbon to give a festive finishing touch.

This particular blend of mincemeat keeps well and provides an excellent filling for mince pies.

Preparation time: 20 minutes, plus standing
Cooking time: about 15 minutes
50 cals per 15 ml (1 tbsp)
Makes about 1.8 kg (4 lb)

550 g (1¼ lb) cooking apples

butter

50 g (2 oz) walnut pieces

125 g (4 oz) blanched almonds

225 g (8 oz) each seedless raisins, sultanas and currants

125 g (4 oz) mixed peel

225 g (8 oz) soft dark brown sugar

grated rind and juice of 1 lemon

grated rind and juice of 1 orange

5 ml (1 tsp) ground cinnamon

2.5 ml (½ tsp) each ground nutmeg and ginger

pinch ground cloves

125 g (4 oz) vegetable suet

150 ml (5 fl oz) brandy

1 Peel, core and roughly chop the apples. Place in a saucepan with 60 ml (4 tbsp) water and a knob of butter. Cook, uncovered, over a low heat until very soft and mushy. Uncover and cook, stirring, over a high heat for 2-3 minutes, or until there is very little excess liquid. Transfer to a bowl and allow to cool.

2 Roughly chop the walnuts and almonds, then place together in a large bowl with all the remaining ingredients. Stir in the cold apple purée. Cover and leave the mixture to stand overnight.

3 Stir the mincemeat mixture well before spooning into sterilised jars. Press down well to exclude any air, then seal. Store in a cool dark place for up to 6 months.

Freezing: not suitable

Bottled Spiced Pears, Peaches and Nectarines

Beautiful bottled fruits – picked when in their prime and poached in a sweet-sour and spiced sugar syrup – make lovely Christmas gifts. They are particularly delicious served with hot or cold ham. Use whole spices for optimum flavour and effect.

Preparation time: 20 minutes
Cooking time: about 20 minutes
55 cals per serving
Makes 900 g (2 lb)

900 g (2 lb) ripe but firm unblemished William pears

2.5 cm (1 inch) piece fresh root ginger

1 lemon

450 g (1 lb) golden granulated sugar

300 ml (10 fl oz) white wine vinegar

300 ml (10 fl oz) clear malt vinegar

15 ml (1 tbsp) allspice berries

15 ml (1 tbsp) cloves

1 large cinnamon stick or several pieces of cassia bark

Bottled Spiced Pears, Peaches and Nectarines

1 Carefully peel the pears. Halve or quarter them, then remove the cores. Place in a bowl of water with a little vinegar added to prevent discolouration.

2 Peel and thinly slice the ginger and pare the rind off the lemon in a single strip. Put the sugar and vinegars into a saucepan and dissolve over a gentle heat. When dissolved, add the ginger, lemon rind, spices and drained pears. Slowly bring to the boil and simmer gently for about 20 minutes or until the pears are just tender – they must remain whole.

3 Lift out the pears with a slotted spoon and pack into sterilised jars, with an even distribution of the cooked spices.

4 Bring the syrup to the boil and boil for 10 minutes or until syrupy. Pour over the pears, making sure they are all covered. Seal and store in a cool dark place for up to 6 months.

Freezing: not suitable

VARIATIONS

For spiced peaches or nectarines, prepare in exactly the same manner, but skin, halve and remove the stones from the fruit. Use orange instead of lemon rind and omit the ginger.

Pumpkin, Apricot and Almond Chutney

A sunny golden chutney to serve with cold meats and cheese, or to offer as a Christmas gift. It must be allowed to mature and mellow for at least one month before using. Pumpkin and apricots go very well together – you will find most greengrocers sell pumpkin by the wedge during autumn and winter.

Preparation time: 30 minutes, plus storing
Cooking time: ¾-1¼ hours
50 cals per 25 g (1 oz)
Makes 1.8 kg (4 lb)

450 g (1 lb) wedge of pumpkin

2 large onions

225 g (8 oz) dried apricots (not no-soak type)

600 ml (1 pint) cider vinegar

450 g (1 lb) soft light brown (muscovado) sugar

225 g (8 oz) sultanas

finely grated rind and juice of 1 orange

30 ml (2 tbsp) salt

2.5 ml (½ tsp) turmeric

2 cardamom pods, crushed

5 ml (1 tsp) mild chilli seasoning

10 ml (2 tsp) coriander seeds

125 g (4 oz) blanched almonds

1 Remove any seeds from the pumpkin and cut off the skin. Cut the flesh into 2.5 cm (1 inch) cubes. Peel and slice the onions. Cut the dried apricots into chunks.

2 Place the vinegar and sugar in a large heavy-based saucepan and bring to the boil. Add the pumpkin, dried apricots and onions, together with all the remaining ingredients, except the almonds. Stir the mixture well and bring to the boil.

3 Turn down the heat and cook gently until soft and thick, stirring occasionally whilst runny, but more frequently as the chutney thickens. Do not let it catch and burn. The mixture may take between 45 minutes and 1¼ hours to thicken and cook; don't let it become too dry. To test, draw a wooden spoon through the mixture – it should leave a clear trail at the bottom of the pan which fills up slowly.

4 Stir in the almonds and pack the chutney into warm sterilised jars (it won't matter if they are still wet). Seal and store in a cool dark place for at least 1 month before using.

Freezing: not suitable

VARIATION

Prune and Apple Chutney: Use 450 g (1 lb) cooking apples and 225 g (8 oz) stoned prunes in place of the pumpkin and apricots. Substitute lemon, raisins and walnuts for the orange, sultanas and almonds. Instead of the spices listed, use 10 ml (2 tsp) mustard seeds, 1 cinnamon stick and 3 cloves.

SUPPLIERS OF CHRISTMAS DECORATIONS AND MATERIALS

British Christmas Tree Growers Association
12 Lauriston Road
London
SW19 4TQ
0181-946 2695
List of tree plantations around the country and further information on the care of Christmas trees available by sending a large SAE.

Candle Makers Supplies
28 Blythe Road
London
W14 0HA
0171-602 4031
Do-it-yourself candle making kits, and a wide selection of candles including church, beeswax, novelty and fruit shapes.

C M Offray & Son Limited
Firtree Place
Church Road
Ashford
Middlesex
TW15 2PH
01784-247281
Ribbon specialists. An extensive ribbon collection in many colours and widths. Call for stockists nationwide.

Coats Crafts
P O Box 22
The Lingfield Estate
McMullen Road
Darlington
DL1 1YQ
01325-394394
Wave cutters to edge paper, paper punch cutters and other craft materials. Call for nationwide stockists.

Davenports Magic Shop
7 Charing Cross Shopping Arcade
The Strand
London
WC2N 4HZ
0171-836 0408
Suppliers of snaps for crackers. Also available by mail order.

Fast Flowers
609 Fulham Road
London
SW6 5UA
0171-381 6422
Florist. Mary Jane Vaughan designed and made the fresh heart wreath featured on page 24.

John Lewis Partnership
Oxford Street
London
W1A 1EX
0171-629 7711
In the haberdashery, fabric and craft departments, look out for beads, buttons, feathers, upholstery tacks, polystyrene balls, chenille yarn, felt, hessian, calico, selection of glue and scissors. Also a good selection of fake fir garlands and twig wreaths. Call for branches nationwide.

Neal Street East
5 Neal Street
London
WC2H 9PU
0171-240 0135
Good selection of novelty and small gifts for crackers.

Paperchase
213 Tottenham Court Road
London
W1P 9AF
0171-580 8496
A wide selection of decorative paper, cards, raffia, craft materials, fake garlands and wreaths and Christmas tree decorations. Mail order catalogue available.

Pavilion
6A Howe Street
Edinburgh
EH3 6TD
0131-225 3590
Stencils and paints. Mail order catalogue available.

Price's Candles
110 York Road
London
SW11 3RU
0171-228 3345
Candle specialists. There is a retail shop at this address, but Price's candles are available nationwide from department stores, gift shops and supermarkets.

Robert Dyas
35 Imperial Way
Croydon
Surrey
CR0 4RR
0181-681 0311
Stock Hilton's button polish for varnishing papier-mâché. Call for branches nationwide.

Stephen Woodhams
60 Ledbury Road
London
W11
0171-243 3141
Architectural garden designer and florist. He designed and made the traditional fresh garland featured on page 22.

Specialist Crafts
P O Box 247
Leicester
LE1 9QS
0116-251 0405
Arts and crafts materials by mail order.

The English Stamp Company
Sunnydown
Worth Matravers
Dorset
BH19 3JP
01929-439117
Stamps and paints by mail order.

The Stamping Ground
P O Box 1364
London
W5 5ZH
0181-758 8629
Stamps and paints by mail order.

The Stencil Library
Stocksfield Hall
Stocksfield
Northumberland
NE43 7TN
01661-844844
Stencils and paints by mail order. Designs also made to order.

V V Rouleaux
10 Symons Street
London
SW3 2TJ
0171-730 3125
Fax: 0171-730 3468
Ribbon specialists. An extensive selection of ribbon including wire-edge, cord, tassles and trimmings in plain colours as well as tartan and other motifs. The shop is based at this address, but orders can also be dealt with by fax or letter.

INDEX